AF490284

ENGLISH COMPANION FOR EUPHONY

PRESCRIBED FOR 1ST SEMESTER BBA AND BCA - SEP BY UNIVERSITY OF MYSORE

DR. SHALINI S.

Copyright © Dr. Shalini S.
All Rights Reserved.

This book has been self-published with all reasonable efforts taken to make the material error-free by the author. No part of this book shall be used, reproduced in any manner whatsoever without written permission from the author, except in the case of brief quotations embodied in critical articles and reviews.

The Author of this book is solely responsible and liable for its content including but not limited to the views, representations, descriptions, statements, information, opinions and references ["Content"]. The Content of this book shall not constitute or be construed or deemed to reflect the opinion or expression of the Publisher or Editor. Neither the Publisher nor Editor endorse or approve the Content of this book or guarantee the reliability, accuracy or completeness of the Content published herein and do not make any representations or warranties of any kind, express or implied, including but not limited to the implied warranties of merchantability, fitness for a particular purpose. The Publisher and Editor shall not be liable whatsoever for any errors, omissions, whether such errors or omissions result from negligence, accident, or any other cause or claims for loss or damages of any kind, including without limitation, indirect or consequential loss or damage arising out of use, inability to use, or about the reliability, accuracy or sufficiency of the information contained in this book.

Made with ♥ on the Notion Press Platform
www.notionpress.com

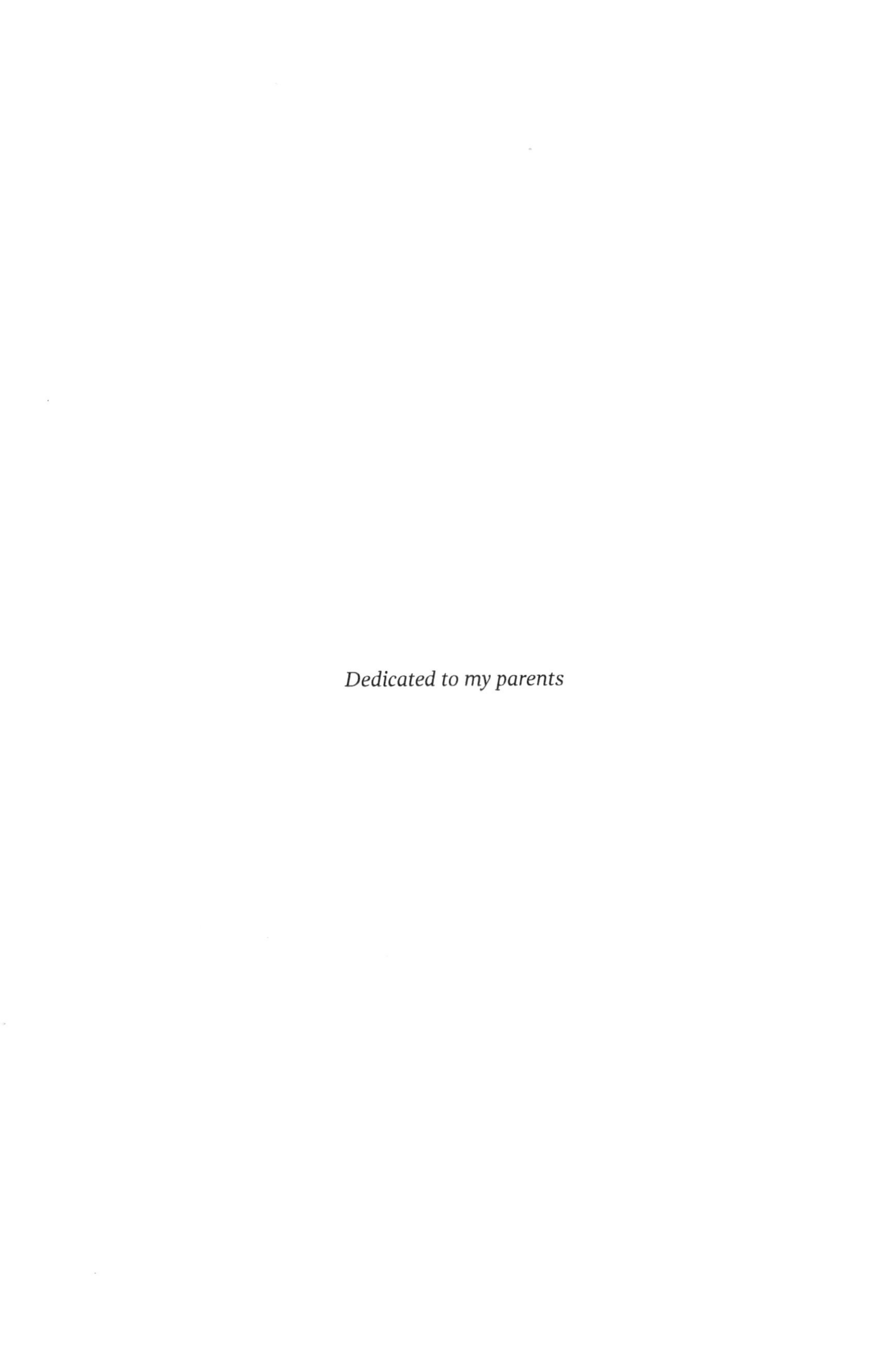

Dedicated to my parents

Contents

Preface

vii

Dear Readers,

This is a carefully drafted book that caters to your first year degree requirements.

Being my third book, all the feedback, input and inspirations I have received from my earlier ventures have been incorporated in this book so as to make it very convenient yet elaborate, both from the exam perspective as well knowledge gaining.

I am sure you will be best benefited from this book; your feedback will motivate me into publishing my next.

Your views can be shared on my email ID shalini.s1982@gmail.com

Happy academics.

Dr. Shalini S.
Assistant Professor
Sapient College of Commerce and Management
Mysore

Acknowledgements

I recently concluded my journey of research scholarship to earn my doctoral title, however the journey is far from over as I am spontaneously reaping benefits from the journey by way of motivation, inspiration and newer challenges. This book is also a result of my past journey and I dedicate this book to all the well-wishers who have been constantly supporting me in every assignment I sign up to.

Professor Gajanan who has remained my guide through my PhD years and continues to guide me in every walk of life deserves my first and foremost thanks for navigating me through my venture into authoring.

Professor Shareef who has always been a constant support for me for over a decade now, took up the task of proofreading the entire content to enhance the vocabulary and make it error-free.

I am grateful for the management and my higher-ups of Sapient College of Commerce and Management, for giving me an opportunity to publish this academic book.

On a personal front, if I am what I am today, it is because of my beloved husband Ravindra who has always held my hand during difficult times and has been there as a strong support in every assignment I have completed.

Dr. Shalini S

CHAPTER ONE

AUTHOR BRIEF

1. **William Shakespeare (1564-1616)**

   William Shakespeare, often referred to as the Bard of Avon, is one of the most influential playwrights and poets in English literature. His works, including plays like "Hamlet," "Romeo and Juliet," and "Macbeth," have had a profound impact on literature and drama. Shakespeare's writing is renowned for its rich language, complex characters, and exploration of universal themes such as love, power, and betrayal.

2. **John Milton (1608-1674)**

   John Milton was an English poet and intellectual best known for his epic poem "Paradise Lost," which explores the biblical story of the Fall of Man. Milton's work is celebrated for its epic grandeur, intricate verse, and deep theological and philosophical insights. His writings have influenced both literature and political thought.

3. **Henry Wadsworth Longfellow (1807-1882)**

   Henry Wadsworth Longfellow was an American poet and educator known for his lyric poetry and works such as "The Song of Hiawatha" and "Paul Revere's Ride." His poetry often reflected themes of American history and folklore, and he was one of the most popular poets of his time in the United States.

4. **Seamus Heaney (1939-2013)**

   Seamus Heaney was an Irish poet, playwright, and translator who received the Nobel Prize in Literature in 1995. His poetry is known for its exploration of Irish rural life, history, and conflict, with notable collections including "Death of a Naturalist" and "The Spirit Level." Heaney's work is celebrated for its rich imagery and lyrical quality.

5. **D.H. Lawrence (1885-1930)**

   D.H. Lawrence was an English novelist, poet, and essayist whose works often explored themes of sexuality, emotional health, and the relationship between the individual and society. His notable works include "Sons and Lovers," "Women in Love," and "Lady Chatterley's Lover." Lawrence's writing is known for its bold exploration of human relationships and psychological complexity.

6. **Alice Walker (b. 1944)**

   Alice Walker is an American author and activist best known for her novel "The Color Purple," which won the Pulitzer Prize for Fiction and the National Book Award. Walker's writing often addresses issues of race, gender, and social injustice, and she is renowned for her contributions to African American literature and feminist thought.

7. **O. Henry (1862-1910)**

   O. Henry was the pen name of William Sydney Porter, an American short story writer known for his witty, ironic, and often surprising endings. His stories, such as "The Gift of the Magi" and "The Ransom of Red Chief," are celebrated for their clever plots and rich characterizations.

8. **A.J. Cronin (1896-1981)**

   A.J. Cronin was a Scottish novelist and physician whose works often explored themes of social justice and human compassion. His best-known novels include "The Citadel," "The Stars Look Down," and "Dr. Finlay's Casebook." Cronin's writing is noted for its vivid storytelling and social commentary.

9. **K.A. Abbas (1914-1987)**

   K.A. Abbas was an Indian writer, journalist, and filmmaker known for his short stories and novels that often reflect the social and political issues of post-independence India. His works include "The Road," "Inquilab," and "The Householder." Abbas's writing is recognized for its insightful portrayal of contemporary Indian society.

10. **A.G. Gardiner (1865-1946)**

    A.G. Gardiner was an English journalist and essayist known for his clear, engaging prose and thoughtful commentary on social issues. His essays, collected in volumes such as "The Common Touch," often address topics ranging from politics to everyday life with a blend of humor and insight.

11. **Jawaharlal Nehru (1889-1964)**

    Jawaharlal Nehru was the first Prime Minister of India and a prominent figure in Indian politics and literature. His writings, including "The Discovery of India," reflect his deep engagement with Indian history, culture, and politics. Nehru's works are valued for their historical perspective and political insight.

12. **Amitav Ghosh (b. 1956)**

Amitav Ghosh is an Indian author known for his novels that explore themes of history, culture, and migration. His notable works include "The Shadow Lines," "The Glass Palace," and "Sea of Poppies." Ghosh's writing is distinguished by its rich narrative style and its examination of the interconnectedness of global histories and cultures.

CHAPTER TWO

LET ME NOT TO THE MARRIAGE OF TRUE MINDS (SONNET 116)

• **William Shakespeare**

Let me not to the marriage of true minds
Admit impediments; love is not love
Which alters when it alteration finds,
Or bends with the remover to remove.
O no, it is an ever-fixèd mark
That looks on tempests and is never shaken;
It is the star to every wand'ring bark
Whose worth's unknown, although his height be taken.
Love's not time's fool, though rosy lips and cheeks
Within his bending sickle's compass come.
Love alters not with his brief hours and weeks,
But bears it out even to the edge of doom:
If this be error and upon me proved,
I never writ, nor no man ever loved.

Line 1: "Let me not to the marriage of true minds"

Summary: The speaker begins by declaring that he will not allow any obstacles to interfere with the union of two minds that are truly in sync and united in love.

Analysis: Shakespeare uses the metaphor of "marriage" to signify a perfect and ideal union. The "true minds" represent a genuine and deep connection between two people, suggesting that their bond is intellectual and spiritual, not just physical.

Line 2: "Admit impediments. Love is not love"

Summary: The speaker insists that true love does not acknowledge any obstacles or impediments that might arise.

Analysis: The term "impediments" refers to the barriers or objections that might be raised during a marriage ceremony (as in traditional vows). Shakespeare asserts that real love cannot be altered by any external factors; if it can, then it is not true love.

Line 3: "Which alters when it alteration finds,"

Summary: True love does not change even when circumstances around it change.

Analysis: Shakespeare is emphasizing the constancy of true love. If love changes when the situation changes, then it is not genuine. The idea is that true love remains steadfast, irrespective of external factors.

Line 4: "Or bends with the remover to remove:"

Summary: True love does not waver or disappear when someone tries to take it away or when difficulties arise.

Analysis: The metaphor of "bending" suggests that false love is weak and malleable, easily distorted by external pressures. Shakespeare's view is that true love is strong and unyielding, not susceptible to such influences.

Line 5: "O no! it is an ever-fixed mark,"

Summary: True love is a constant and unchanging reference point, much like a lighthouse that guides ships safely to shore.

Analysis: The "ever-fixed mark" is a metaphor for something that is permanent and reliable. In this context, it symbolizes the unwavering nature of true love, which remains steadfast regardless of the challenges it faces.

Line 6: "That looks on tempests and is never shaken;"

Summary: True love can withstand even the most tumultuous storms without being affected.

Analysis: The "tempests" represent life's difficulties and challenges. Shakespeare uses this powerful image to convey that true love remains firm and unshaken, even in the face of adversity.

Line 7: "It is the star to every wandering bark,"

Summary: True love is like a guiding star for ships lost at sea, providing direction and hope.

Analysis: The "wandering bark" (a small ship) symbolizes people who are lost or searching for meaning. The "star" is a metaphor for true love, which provides guidance and a sense of purpose, much like the North Star does for sailors.

Line 8: "Whose worth's unknown, although his height be taken."

Summary: Although the star's height can be measured, its true value and significance are beyond understanding.

Analysis: This line reflects the idea that while we can observe and quantify certain aspects of love (or the guiding star), its true essence and worth are immeasurable and transcend simple understanding.

Line 9: "Love's not Time's fool, though rosy lips and cheeks"

Summary: True love is not subject to the ravages of time, even though physical beauty may fade.

Analysis: Shakespeare is asserting that true love is not dependent on physical attributes, which are subject to aging and change. The phrase "Time's fool" suggests that love is not a plaything or victim of time.

Line 10: "Within his bending sickle's compass come:"

Summary: Time may harvest youth and beauty with its "sickle," but true love is not affected by this.

Analysis: The "bending sickle" is a symbol of time's power to bring about decay and death. However, Shakespeare emphasizes that true love transcends physical decay and remains constant.

Line 11: "Love alters not with his brief hours and weeks,"

Summary: True love does not change over time, no matter how much time passes.

Analysis: Shakespeare reiterates the theme of love's constancy by stating that true love is not affected by the passage of time. The use of "brief hours and weeks" highlights the transient nature of time compared to the eternal nature of love.

Line 12: "But bears it out even to the edge of doom."

Summary: True love endures until the end of time, even until the Day of Judgment.

Analysis: The phrase "edge of doom" refers to the end of the world or Judgment Day. Shakespeare suggests that true love is eternal and will last until the very end of time, emphasizing its unyielding nature.

Line 13: "If this be error and upon me proved,"

Summary: The speaker challenges anyone to prove him wrong about his definition of true love.

Analysis: Shakespeare is so confident in his understanding of true love that he invites others to challenge him. This line sets up the concluding couplet, where he stakes his reputation on the truth of his statements.

Line 14: "I never writ, nor no man ever loved."

Summary: If his definition of true love is proven wrong, then Shakespeare claims that he has never written anything and that no one has ever truly loved.

Analysis: This final line underscores Shakespeare's conviction. He is so certain of his description of true love that he declares his entire body of work (and the very concept of love) meaningless if he is wrong.

Complete Analysis

Sonnet 116 is one of William Shakespeare's most famous sonnets and is often regarded as a profound exploration of the nature of true love. In this poem, Shakespeare articulates an idealistic view of love, portraying it as constant, unchanging, and unaffected by time or circumstances.

The sonnet begins by establishing what true love is not: it does not change when it encounters obstacles, nor does it waver under pressure. Shakespeare uses metaphors like the "ever-fixed mark" and the "star to every wandering bark" to illustrate the steadfastness and guidance that true love provides. These images convey the idea that love, like a lighthouse or the North Star, is a reliable and enduring force that helps navigate the challenges of life.

Shakespeare then contrasts true love with the effects of time. While physical beauty may fade ("rosy lips and cheeks"), true love is not "Time's fool" and does not alter with the passage of time. The poet further emphasizes love's eternal nature by asserting that it "bears it out even to the edge of doom," suggesting that true love will endure until the very end of time.

The closing couplet serves as a bold declaration of the poet's belief in his definition of love. Shakespeare challenges anyone to prove him wrong, stating that if he is mistaken, then all his writings are false, and the very concept of love is nonexistent.

Overall, Sonnet 116 is a celebration of love's permanence and resilience. It presents an idealized view of love that transcends physical attraction, time, and circumstance. Shakespeare's eloquent portrayal of love's constancy has made this sonnet a timeless piece of literature, often quoted in discussions of romantic and marital commitment.

Important Questions and Answers:

Question 1: What is the central theme of Sonnet 116?

The central theme of Sonnet 116 is the constancy and unchanging nature of true love. Shakespeare presents an idealized view of love, suggesting that it is not subject to change, decay, or the passage of time. According to the poet, true love does not alter when circumstances change or when challenges arise; rather, it remains steadfast and enduring. Shakespeare uses metaphors such as the "ever-fixed mark" and the "star to every wandering bark" to illustrate this concept of love as a reliable and guiding force. The poem also contrasts true love with the effects of time, asserting that while physical beauty may fade, true love does not succumb to time's influence. Ultimately, the poem suggests that true love is eternal, surviving "even to the edge of doom," or the end of time. This portrayal of love as unwavering and permanent serves as a powerful exploration of the ideal qualities of love, emphasizing its spiritual and emotional depth over superficial, physical attraction. Shakespeare's depiction of love as an unbreakable bond between "true minds" has resonated through the ages, making Sonnet 116 one of his most celebrated works on the subject of love.

Question 2: How does Shakespeare use metaphors in Sonnet 116 to convey the nature of true love?

Shakespeare employs powerful metaphors throughout Sonnet 116 to convey the steadfast and unchanging nature of true love. One of the most significant metaphors is the "ever-fixed mark," which likens true love to a lighthouse or a guiding beacon that remains constant and unyielding, no matter how turbulent the seas may be. This image suggests that true love is a reliable force that offers guidance and stability, even in the face of life's challenges. Another key metaphor is the "star to every wandering bark," where true love is compared to the North Star, which has traditionally been used by sailors to navigate their way. This metaphor emphasizes love's role as a guiding light, helping individuals find their way through the uncertainties of life. Additionally, Shakespeare contrasts true love with the effects of time, using the image of "Time's fool" to illustrate that true love is not subject to the ravages of time. Unlike physical beauty, which is susceptible to decay, true love endures. Shakespeare's metaphors work together to create a portrait of love as a powerful, unchanging force that transcends the physical world, emphasizing its spiritual and emotional aspects. These metaphors enrich the poem's message, reinforcing the idea that true love is eternal and unshakeable, regardless of external circumstances.

Question 3: How does Shakespeare depict the relationship between love and time in Sonnet 116?

In Sonnet 116, Shakespeare presents a complex relationship between love and time, emphasizing that true love is immune to the passage of time and the changes it brings. He explicitly states that "Love's not Time's fool," meaning that true love is not at the mercy of time's inevitable effects, such as aging and decay. This assertion suggests that while time may alter physical attributes like "rosy lips and cheeks," it has no power over the essence of true love, which remains constant and unchanging. Shakespeare further explores this idea by referring to time's "bending sickle," a metaphor for the way time harvests youth and beauty. Despite this, true love "alters not with his brief hours and weeks," indicating that love does not diminish as time passes. Instead, it endures until "the edge of doom," or the end of time itself. Through this depiction, Shakespeare elevates love to a timeless, almost eternal force that defies the limitations imposed by time. By asserting that true love is unaffected by the natural progression of time, the poet challenges the notion that love is tied to physical beauty or youth, instead portraying it as a deep, spiritual connection that outlasts all temporal concerns. This portrayal reinforces the sonnet's overall theme of love's constancy and serves as a testament to its enduring power.

Question 4: What does Shakespeare mean by the phrase "the marriage of true minds" in Sonnet 116?

The phrase "the marriage of true minds" in Sonnet 116 refers to the union of two people who are perfectly aligned in thought, understanding, and love. Shakespeare uses this metaphorical expression to suggest that true love is a deep connection between individuals that goes beyond physical attraction or superficial compatibility. The "marriage" here symbolizes an ideal, spiritual bond that is based on mutual respect, intellectual compatibility, and unwavering loyalty. By focusing on the union of "minds" rather than bodies, Shakespeare emphasizes that true love is rooted in a profound understanding and acceptance of one another, rather than being based on fleeting or external qualities. This concept of love as a "marriage of true minds" implies that true love is unbreakable and eternal, not subject to change or dissolution, even in the face of challenges. It also suggests that such a union is rare and precious, something that should be cherished and protected from any "impediments." In essence, the phrase encapsulates the sonnet's overarching theme that true love is an unchanging and enduring force, one that cannot be altered by external circumstances or the passage of time. This idealized view of love as a meeting of minds, rather than just hearts or bodies, highlights the depth and permanence of the bond that Shakespeare envisions.

Question 5: How does the concluding couplet of Sonnet 116 reinforce the poet's message about true love?

The concluding couplet of Sonnet 116—"If this be error and upon me proved, / I never writ, nor no man ever loved"—serves as a powerful reinforcement of the poet's message about the nature of true love. In these final lines, Shakespeare makes a bold declaration, asserting that if anyone can prove him wrong in his depiction of love, then all his writings are false, and the very concept of love is a myth. This hyperbolic statement underscores the poet's absolute confidence in his definition of true love as constant, unchanging, and eternal. By staking his entire literary reputation on the truth of his assertions, Shakespeare elevates the importance of the sonnet's message, implying that the principles of love he has outlined are universal truths. The use of the word "error" suggests that any deviation from this idealized view of love would be a fundamental misunderstanding of what love truly is. The couplet also serves to challenge the reader, inviting them to reflect on their own experiences and understanding of love. Shakespeare's willingness to dismiss all of his work if his view of love is incorrect emphasizes the gravity and significance of the poem's theme. This rhetorical flourish not only reinforces the sonnet's message but also leaves a lasting impression on the reader, cementing the idea that true love is an enduring and unassailable force, beyond the reach of time, circumstance, or even doubt.

CHAPTER THREE

ON HIS BLINDNESS

• **John Milton**

John Milton's sonnet "On His Blindness" is a profound reflection on the poet's experience of blindness and his relationship with God. The poem, written in the Petrarchan (Italian) sonnet form, is composed of an octave (the first eight lines) and a sestet (the last six lines). Below is a stanza-wise summary and analysis of the sonnet.

Text:

When I consider how my light is spent,
Ere half my days, in this dark world and wide,
And that one Talent which is death to hide
Lodged with me useless, though my Soul more bent
To serve therewith my Maker, and present
My true account, lest he returning chide;
"Doth God exact day-labour, light denied?"
I fondly ask. But patience, to prevent
That murmur, soon replies, "God doth not need
Either man's work or his own gifts; who best
Bear his mild yoke, they serve him best. His state
Is Kingly. Thousands at his bidding speed
And post o'er Land and Ocean without rest:
They also serve who only stand and wait."

Stanza 1 (Lines 1-8): The Octave

Summary:

The speaker reflects on how his "light" (a metaphor for his eyesight) has been spent and lost before he could accomplish his life's work, which he believes was intended to serve God. He laments that he is now "dark," unable to use the talents that God has given him. The speaker worries that God will judge him harshly for being unable to perform the duties that were expected of him. He fears that his blindness might make him useless in the service of God and wonders how he can fulfill his purpose if he can no longer see.

Analysis:

The octave of the sonnet is characterized by the speaker's deep concern over the loss of his sight and the implications this has for his spiritual and creative life. The phrase "light is spent" symbolizes both Milton's physical blindness and the fading of his creative powers. The use of the word "spent" suggests that his eyesight was a resource that has now been exhausted. The poet's reference to the "one talent" alludes to the biblical parable of the talents, where servants are entrusted with money to invest by their master. In Milton's case, his talent is his ability to write and serve God through his poetry. The fear of being judged by God for not using this talent is at the heart of his anxiety. This stanza captures the poet's struggle with the idea of divine justice, as he grapples with the apparent unfairness of his situation. The mood of the octave is one of despair and confusion, as the speaker wrestles with the implications of his blindness on his purpose in life.

Stanza 2 (Lines 9-14): The Sestet

Summary:

In the sestet, the speaker's tone shifts from despair to acceptance. He realizes that God does not require "man's work" or the use of talents in a conventional sense. Instead, God values patience and the willingness to serve Him in whatever capacity one can. The speaker concludes that those who "stand and wait" are also serving God, even if they are not actively doing physical work. This realization brings the speaker peace, as he understands that his worth in God's eyes is not diminished by his blindness.

Analysis:

The sestet marks a turning point in the poem, where the speaker moves from questioning God's justice to accepting His will. The personification of "Patience" in line 8, which responds to the speaker's concerns, symbolizes the inner voice of reason and faith. This voice reassures the speaker that God's requirements are not as he feared; God does not need human beings to perform specific tasks but rather to have faith and trust in His plan. The famous line "They also serve who only stand and wait" suggests that passive acceptance of God's will is also a form of service. This idea is deeply rooted in Christian theology, where obedience and submission to God's will are seen as virtuous. The sestet thus provides a resolution to the speaker's inner turmoil, offering a message of hope and reassurance. The poet's realization that he can still serve God despite his blindness reflects Milton's own struggle with his disability and his faith. The tone of the sestet is one of calm and acceptance, contrasting with the anxiety of the octave.

Complete Analysis

John Milton's "On His Blindness" is a poignant meditation on the challenges of faith in the face of personal adversity. The sonnet reflects Milton's own experience of becoming blind in middle age and the spiritual crisis that this provoked. The poem is structured as a Petrarchan sonnet, with the octave presenting a problem or concern and the sestet providing a resolution or answer.

In the octave, Milton expresses his deep frustration and fear that his blindness has rendered him useless in the service of God. He worries that his inability to use his poetic talent might lead to divine condemnation, as he fears that he has failed to fulfill his purpose. This reflects the poet's inner conflict and his struggle to reconcile his disability with his faith.

The sestet offers a resolution to this conflict through the voice of "Patience." This personified figure represents a comforting and wise perspective, reminding the speaker that God does not demand specific works but values the spirit of obedience and trust. The idea that "They also serve who only stand and wait" is a powerful message of consolation, suggesting that passivity and acceptance are also forms of service to God.

Milton's use of biblical allusions, such as the parable of the talents and the concept of divine justice, adds depth to the poem's exploration of faith and duty. The poem ultimately affirms the idea that one's worth is not determined by their ability to perform certain tasks but by their willingness to accept and trust in God's will.

"On His Blindness" is not just a personal reflection on Milton's own life but also a universal meditation on the nature of service, patience, and faith. It speaks to the human condition of grappling with limitations and the quest for meaning in the face of adversity. The sonnet remains a timeless piece, resonating with anyone who has faced challenges that seem to hinder their ability to fulfill their potential.

Important Questions and Answers:

Question 1: How does Milton's use of the sonnet form contribute to the theme of "On His Blindness"?

Milton's choice of the Petrarchan (Italian) sonnet form in "On His Blindness" plays a significant role in conveying the poem's central theme of faith and resignation. The sonnet consists of 14 lines, divided into an octave (the first eight lines) and a sestet (the final six lines). This structure allows Milton to present a problem or concern in the octave and then resolve or reflect upon it in the sestet.

In the octave, Milton expresses his frustration and anxiety over his blindness, fearing that it has rendered him incapable of serving God. He laments the loss of his "light" and worries that his poetic talent, which he perceives as a gift from God, will go unused. The rigid structure of the sonnet, with its strict rhyme scheme and iambic pentameter, mirrors the poet's feelings of confinement and limitation due to his blindness.

The sestet, however, introduces a shift in tone and perspective. Here, the personified figure of "Patience" responds to Milton's concerns, reminding him that God does not require "man's work" or specific achievements. Instead, what matters is one's willingness to accept God's will and serve in whatever way possible. This resolution in the sestet brings a sense of peace and acceptance to the speaker, reflecting the broader theme of the poem: finding faith and purpose in the face of adversity.

The sonnet form, with its clear division between problem and resolution, underscores the journey from doubt to acceptance that is central to the poem. It allows Milton to explore the tension between his personal struggles and his faith, ultimately conveying a message of hope and trust in divine justice.

Question 2: How does Milton's use of biblical allusions enhance the meaning of "On His Blindness"?

Milton's use of biblical allusions in "On His Blindness" deepens the poem's exploration of faith, service, and divine justice. By drawing on references from the Bible, Milton connects his personal struggle with broader, universally recognized spiritual themes.

One of the most significant allusions is the reference to the parable of the talents, found in the Gospel of Matthew (25:14-30). In the parable, a master entrusts his servants with varying amounts of money ("talents") to invest while he is away. When he returns, he rewards those who have used their talents wisely but punishes the servant who, out of fear, buries his talent and does nothing with it. Milton's fear that he has failed to use his "one talent" effectively mirrors the anxiety of the unproductive servant in the parable. This allusion underscores Milton's concern that his blindness might prevent him from fulfilling his God-given purpose, thus leading to divine disapproval.

Another allusion in the poem is the personification of "Patience," which can be seen as a reference to the Christian virtue of patience, as emphasized in the Bible. Patience, as a Christian virtue, is often associated with enduring suffering and waiting for God's will to unfold. In the poem, Patience reassures Milton that God does not demand specific works but values the willingness to serve and accept His will. This reflects the biblical message that faith and obedience are more important than outward achievements.

These biblical allusions enhance the poem's meaning by situating Milton's personal experience within a larger spiritual context. They allow the poem to resonate not just as an individual lament but as a meditation on universal themes of duty, faith, and divine justice.

Question 3: What role does the personification of "Patience" play in the resolution of Milton's internal conflict in "On His Blindness"?

The personification of "Patience" in "On His Blindness" plays a crucial role in resolving the internal conflict that Milton experiences due to his blindness. Throughout the octave, Milton expresses deep anxiety and frustration, fearing that his loss of sight has rendered him unable to fulfill his divine purpose. He worries that he is unable to use his poetic talent, which he believes was given to him by God for a specific purpose. This concern leads to a crisis of faith, as Milton questions how he can serve God if he is no longer able to see.

The introduction of "Patience" in the sestet marks a turning point in the poem. Patience is personified as a comforting and wise voice that responds to Milton's fears and offers a different perspective. This figure reassures Milton that God does not require specific works or achievements from His followers. Instead, what matters is one's willingness to serve and accept God's will, regardless of the circumstances. Patience tells Milton that "They also serve who only stand and wait," suggesting that even passive acceptance and trust in God's plan are forms of service.

The personification of Patience thus provides a resolution to Milton's inner turmoil. It helps him realize that his worth in God's eyes is not diminished by his blindness. Instead of focusing on what he cannot do, Milton is encouraged to embrace the idea that his faith and willingness to serve are what truly matter. This shift in perspective brings the poem to a peaceful and accepting conclusion, with Milton finding solace in the understanding that God values his patience and faith just as much as any active service he might have performed.

Question 4: How does the theme of divine justice manifest in Milton's "On His Blindness"?

The theme of divine justice is central to John Milton's "On His Blindness," as the poet grapples with his loss of sight and its implications for his relationship with God. Throughout the sonnet, Milton reflects on the fairness of his situation and the nature of God's expectations for human service.

In the octave, Milton's concern about divine justice is evident in his fear that God will judge him harshly for being unable to use his poetic talent due to his blindness. He worries that he is not fulfilling the purpose for which he was created, which leads to anxiety about how he will be judged by God. The poet's reference to the "one talent" he has been given and his concern about being found wanting allude to the biblical parable of the talents, where servants are judged based on how well they use the resources entrusted to them. Milton's fear reflects his struggle to understand how divine justice applies to his situation, given his physical limitations.

However, the sestet provides a resolution to this concern by offering a different perspective on divine justice. Through the personified figure of "Patience," Milton comes to understand that God's justice is not based solely on human achievements or works. Instead, it is grounded in the recognition of one's circumstances and the willingness to accept and serve God's will. Patience reassures Milton that "God doth not need / Either man's work or his own gifts," implying that divine justice is not about punishing those who cannot perform specific tasks but about valuing the spirit of faith and submission.

In this way, the theme of divine justice in "On His Blindness" is ultimately one of reassurance and comfort. Milton comes to realize that God's justice is compassionate and understanding, taking into account human limitations and valuing the intent and faith behind one's actions rather than the actions themselves. This understanding brings the poet peace and helps him reconcile his blindness with his faith in God's just and benevolent nature.

Question 5: How does "On His Blindness" reflect Milton's personal struggles and his faith?

"On His Blindness" is deeply reflective of John Milton's personal struggles, particularly his experience with blindness and how it affected his faith and sense of purpose. Milton became completely blind by 1652, and this physical affliction profoundly impacted his life and work. The sonnet serves as a window into his internal conflict as he grapples with the implications of his blindness on his ability to serve God through his writing.

In the poem, Milton expresses his fear that his blindness has rendered him useless, particularly in fulfilling what he believes to be his divine purpose. The loss of his "light" symbolizes not only his physical sight but also his creative vision and ability to contribute meaningfully to the world. This concern is especially poignant for Milton, who saw his poetry as a way to glorify God. The reference to his "one talent" being "lodged with me useless" underscores his anxiety about wasting the gifts God has bestowed upon him, which he feels unable to utilize due to his blindness.

However, the poem also reflects Milton's deep faith and his eventual acceptance of God's will. Through the personified figure of "Patience," Milton comes to realize that his worth is not determined by his ability to produce work or achieve specific goals, but by his willingness to accept his condition and serve God in whatever way he can. The poem's conclusion, "They also serve who only stand and wait," reflects Milton's acceptance of his blindness as part of God's plan, and his belief that even in his state of physical darkness, he can still serve a divine purpose.

Thus, "On His Blindness" encapsulates Milton's personal struggle with his physical limitations while also showcasing his unwavering faith. The sonnet moves from a place of doubt and fear to one of acceptance and spiritual understanding, making it a powerful reflection of Milton's inner life and his relationship with God.

CHAPTER FOUR

A PSALM OF LIFE

• Henry Wadsworth Longfellow

Tell me not, in mournful numbers,
Life is but an empty dream!
For the soul is dead that slumbers,
And things are not what they seem.
Life is real! Life is earnest!
And the grave is not its goal;
Dust thou art, to dust returnest,
Was not spoken of the soul.
Not enjoyment, and not sorrow,
Is our destined end or way;
But to act, that each to-morrow
Find us farther than to-day.
Art is long, and Time is fleeting,
And our hearts, though stout and brave,
Still, like muffled drums, are beating
Funeral marches to the grave.
In the world's broad field of battle,
In the bivouac of Life,
Be not like dumb, driven cattle!
Be a hero in the strife!
Trust no Future, howe'er pleasant!
Let the dead Past bury its dead!
Act,— act in the living Present!
Heart within, and God o'erhead!

Lives of great men all remind us
We can make our lives sublime,
And, departing, leave behind us
Footprints on the sands of time;
Footprints, that perhaps another,
Sailing o'er life's solemn main,
A forlorn and shipwrecked brother,
Seeing, shall take heart again.
Let us, then, be up and doing,
With a heart for any fate;
Still achieving, still pursuing,
Learn to labor and to wait.

Stanza 1:*Summary:*

In the opening stanza, the poet addresses the "Psalmist" and urges him not to convey a sad and mournful perspective on life. Instead of seeing life as an empty dream, the poet asserts that life is real, substantial, and has a purpose. The notion that life is an illusion or mere prelude to death is rejected.

Analysis:

Longfellow begins the poem by challenging the melancholic view often associated with religious hymns or psalms. He emphasizes the value of life, rejecting the idea that it is insignificant or a mere stepping stone to the afterlife. By stating "Life is real! Life is earnest!" the poet highlights the seriousness and significance of our earthly existence. The rejection of the phrase "dust thou art, to dust returnest" symbolizes a defiance against the fatalistic acceptance of death as the only end, urging instead a focus on the vitality of life.

Stanza 2:*Summary:*

The poet continues by dismissing the notion that life is a dream or an illusion. He argues that life is not an empty or purposeless journey, and each moment carries weight and meaning. Life is not merely a time to prepare for the afterlife; it is a time for action and fulfillment.

Analysis:

Here, Longfellow builds on the idea that life is not just a passage toward death. The phrase "not enjoyment, and not sorrow" emphasizes that life should not be reduced to mere emotions or states of being. Life is meant for action, progress, and self-realization. This stanza serves as a call to embrace the reality of life, to live actively and with intention, rather than passively awaiting an inevitable end.

Stanza 3:*Summary:*

Longfellow draws a clear distinction between life and death, asserting that the purpose of life is not to succumb to death but to achieve something meaningful. Life is short, and the heart is still alive and beating, full of vigor and vitality. The poet urges the reader to make the most of life's fleeting nature.

Analysis:

The poet's use of the metaphor "Art is long, and Time is fleeting" underscores the idea that while life is temporary, the impact of our actions can endure. The heart, symbolizing human emotion and drive, is described as "stout and brave," signifying the strength and courage needed to live a meaningful life. This stanza stresses the importance of making every moment count, as time is limited but the legacy one leaves behind can be eternal.

Stanza 4:*Summary:*

The poet reminds the reader that life is not just about pleasure or sorrow, but about actively striving to make a difference. The actions we take in life shape our character and destiny. The poet advises against becoming discouraged by failures or elated by successes, urging a balanced and resilient approach to life.

Analysis:

In this stanza, Longfellow emphasizes the importance of maintaining a balanced perspective on life. The advice to "be not like dumb, driven cattle" suggests that one should not blindly follow the crowd but should instead forge their own path with determination and purpose. The call to "act in the living present" encourages readers to focus on the present moment, seizing opportunities and taking control of their own lives.

Stanza 5:*Summary:*

Longfellow continues to emphasize the importance of living a life of purpose. He encourages the reader to leave behind a legacy that will inspire others, suggesting that our lives should be examples for those who come after us. The poet urges us to strive for greatness and to leave "footprints on the sands of time."

Analysis:

This stanza is central to the poem's message. The metaphor of "footprints on the sands of time" symbolizes the lasting impact one can have on the world. By encouraging readers to leave behind a legacy that others can follow, Longfellow emphasizes the idea of life as a journey with the potential for greatness. The footprints represent the positive influence one can have, inspiring others to live meaningful and purposeful lives.

Stanza 6:*Summary:*

The poet speaks to the idea of perseverance, urging the reader not to lose heart even in the face of challenges. He acknowledges that life is full of obstacles but encourages a mindset of resilience and determination. Life's journey may be difficult, but the goal is to keep moving forward with faith and courage.

Analysis:

Longfellow's use of the phrase "A forlorn and shipwrecked brother" evokes the image of someone who has faced great adversity. However, the poet's message is one of hope and encouragement, suggesting that by persevering through difficult times, one can still achieve a meaningful and impactful life. The stanza reinforces the theme of resilience, highlighting the importance of courage and determination in the face of life's inevitable challenges.

Stanza 7: *Summary:*

In the final stanza, the poet reiterates the call to action, urging the reader to live each day to the fullest. The emphasis is on seizing the day ("Act—act in the living Present!") and not dwelling on the past or fearing the future. The poet concludes by encouraging the reader to trust in the higher power and to live a life of action and purpose.

Analysis:

The closing stanza encapsulates the core message of the poem: the importance of living in the present moment with purpose and determination. By urging the reader to "act in the living Present," Longfellow emphasizes the value of the present moment as the only time in which action is possible. The poet's advice to "trust no Future, howe'er pleasant!" and "Let the dead Past bury its dead!" reinforces the idea that one should not be paralyzed by either past regrets or future uncertainties. The poem ends with a call to embrace life with courage and faith, making the most of each day.

Important Questions and Answers:

Question 1: *What is the central message of "A Psalm of Life," and how does Longfellow convey this message through the poem?*

The central message of "A Psalm of Life" is a call to live life with purpose, vigor, and determination. Longfellow rejects the notion that life is merely a prelude to death or an empty dream. Instead, he asserts that life is real and should be lived actively and meaningfully. This message is conveyed through several key elements of the poem.

Firstly, Longfellow uses direct and emphatic language to challenge the traditional, somber view of life. He begins with "Life is real! Life is earnest!" and rejects the idea that life is a mere "empty dream." This rejection sets the tone for the rest of the poem, which emphasizes action and purpose.

Secondly, the poet employs metaphors to illustrate the impact of our actions. For example, "footprints on the sands of time" symbolizes the lasting influence one can have through their deeds. By encouraging readers to make their lives significant, Longfellow highlights the idea that our actions can leave a positive and enduring mark on the world.

Lastly, Longfellow stresses the importance of living in the present and embracing each moment with courage and faith. The advice to "Act—act in the living Present!" underscores the importance of seizing opportunities and making the most of our time. Overall, Longfellow's message is a motivational call to live fully and leave a meaningful legacy.

Question 2: *How does Longfellow use imagery to support the theme of perseverance in "A Psalm of Life"?*

Longfellow uses vivid imagery in "A Psalm of Life" to support the theme of perseverance and the importance of living a purposeful life. The imagery serves to inspire and motivate readers to face challenges with determination and courage.

One prominent example is the metaphor "footprints on the sands of time," which vividly illustrates the idea of leaving a lasting impact through one's actions. The image of footprints suggests that while time may erode the physical traces of our lives, the positive effects of our efforts can endure. This imagery emphasizes that our perseverance and actions can create a legacy that transcends our lifetime.

Additionally, the poem includes the imagery of life as "Art is long, and Time is fleeting." Here, the contrast between "Art" and "Time" underscores the idea that while our time on earth is limited, the achievements and contributions we make can have a lasting impact. The fleeting nature of time contrasts with the enduring quality of meaningful work, reinforcing the need for perseverance in pursuing our goals.

Another evocative image is the portrayal of life as a journey filled with obstacles, where the poet advises not to be like "dumb, driven cattle" but to actively forge one's path. This imagery of navigating a challenging journey underscores the importance of perseverance and active engagement in shaping one's destiny.

Through these images, Longfellow effectively conveys the poem's message about the value of perseverance and the significance of living a life of purpose and action.

CHAPTER FIVE

DIGGING

• Seamus Heancy

Between my finger and my thumb
The squat pen rests; snug as a gun.
Under my window, a clean rasping sound
When the spade sinks into gravelly ground:
My father, digging. I look down
Till his straining rump among the flowerbeds
Bends low, comes up twenty years away
Stooping in rhythm through potato drills
Where he was digging.
The coarse boot nestled on the lug, the shaft
Against the inside knee was levered firmly.
He rooted out tall tops, buried the bright edge deep
To scatter new potatoes that we picked,
Loving their cool hardness in our hands.
By God, the old man could handle a spade.
Just like his old man.
My grandfather cut more turf in a day
Than any other man on Toner's bog.
Once I carried him milk in a bottle
Corked sloppily with paper. He straightened up
To drink it, then fell to right away
Nicking and slicing neatly, heaving sods
Over his shoulder, going down and down
For the good turf. Digging.

The cold smell of potato mould, the squelch and slap
Of soggy peat, the curt cuts of an edge
Through living roots awaken in my head.
But I've no spade to follow men like them.
Between my finger and my thumb
The squat pen rests.
I'll dig with it.

Stanza 1: Summary:

In the opening stanza, the poet reflects on his father's skill as a digger. He describes his father digging up the earth in the garden, with the sound of the spade "squelching" in the ground. The poet admires the physical strength and tradition that his father embodies, highlighting the generational connection to the land and labor.

Analysis:

The stanza sets up the central theme of the poem—roots and heritage. The imagery of the father's physical work and the sounds of digging evoke a sense of deep connection to the land. The use of onomatopoeia ("squelching") enriches the sensory experience of the reader, while the reference to "a gun" subtly suggests a link between manual labor and the poet's own craft of writing. The father's labor symbolizes a lineage of hard work and dedication that the poet both respects and reflects upon.

Stanza 2: Summary:

The poet describes his grandfather's digging skills, noting the precision and craftsmanship of his work. The grandfather's digging is portrayed as part of a long tradition, and his ability to cultivate the land is highlighted. The poet recalls how the grandfather's work was a labor of love, emphasizing his skill and expertise.

Analysis:

In this stanza, Heaney extends the theme of tradition by introducing the grandfather, further anchoring the family's connection to manual labor. The description of the grandfather's work as skillful and passionate underscores the generational continuity in the poet's family. This connection between past and present is central to understanding the poet's identity and his own place in the lineage of his ancestors. The meticulous description of the grandfather's digging acts as a metaphor for the poet's own craft, suggesting a parallel between physical labor and artistic creation.

Stanza 3: Summary:

The poet reflects on his own position as a writer, contrasting his intellectual work with the physical labor of his forefathers. He acknowledges that while he does not engage in physical digging, he is connected to the same tradition through his writing. The poet holds a spade in his hand but sees his pen as a tool for digging deeper into his heritage and identity.

Analysis:

This stanza serves as a pivotal moment of self-reflection for the poet. By juxtaposing his own work as a writer with the physical labor of his ancestors, Heaney explores the theme of heritage and personal identity. The pen becomes a symbolic tool for exploration and excavation of cultural and familial roots. This contrast highlights the shift from physical labor to intellectual labor, yet underscores that both forms of work are deeply rooted in tradition and heritage. The stanza also reflects Heaney's respect for the craftsmanship of his forefathers and his attempt to honor their legacy through his writing.

Stanza 4: Summary:

The poet concludes by contemplating the future, recognizing that his own work, like that of his ancestors, will eventually be seen as part of a larger tradition. He reflects on the cyclical nature of labor and legacy, acknowledging that his writing is a continuation of the work started by his father and grandfather.

Analysis:

In the final stanza, Heaney ties together the themes of tradition, labor, and legacy. The acknowledgment of the cyclical nature of work emphasizes the continuity of family tradition and the poet's role within it. The poem ends with a sense of completion and fulfillment, suggesting that the poet's writing is not a departure from but a continuation of his family's heritage. This reflection highlights the intergenerational connection and the importance of maintaining and honoring one's roots through different forms of work.

Important Questions and Answers

1. How does Seamus Heaney use imagery in "Digging" to convey themes of heritage and labor?

Seamus Heaney employs vivid imagery in "Digging" to underscore the themes of heritage and labor. The sensory details of the father's and grandfather's digging, such as the "squelching" sound of the spade and the tactile experience of the earth, bring the physical labor to life. This imagery not only highlights the skill and dedication of Heaney's ancestors but also emphasizes their deep connection to the land. By describing the meticulous and laborious work of his forefathers, Heaney contrasts it with his own intellectual labor as a writer. The imagery of digging serves as a metaphor for the poet's own process of excavation and exploration of his heritage. Through this comparison, Heaney reflects on the continuity of tradition and the shared value of hard work, bridging the gap between past and present. The detailed portrayal of physical labor thus becomes a powerful symbol of the poet's own creative and reflective process.

2. What role does the pen play in the poem, and how does it relate to the theme of tradition?

In "Digging," the pen is a central symbol that represents the poet's creative and intellectual work. It serves as a contrast to the physical spade used by his father and grandfather, but it also embodies the same principle of digging deeply into one's heritage and identity. The pen is portrayed as a tool for exploration and reflection, akin to the spade's role in cultivating the land. This comparison underscores the theme of tradition by showing that although the nature of labor has changed—from physical digging to writing—the essence of connecting to one's roots remains the same. The poet's use of the pen is an acknowledgment that while he may not engage in manual labor, he continues the legacy of his ancestors through his craft. The pen thus symbolizes a modern continuation of the familial tradition of digging deep into one's roots, linking the poet's work to the enduring values of his heritage.

3. How does Heaney's portrayal of his ancestors' work influence his perception of his own role as a writer?

Heaney's portrayal of his ancestors' work profoundly influences his perception of his own role as a writer. By depicting his father and grandfather as skilled and dedicated laborers, Heaney emphasizes the importance of tradition and craftsmanship. This portrayal leads him to view his own work through a similar lens of commitment and significance. The contrast between the physical labor of digging and his own intellectual labor as a writer highlights the continuity between different forms of work. Heaney perceives his writing as a way of continuing the tradition of deep, meaningful labor established by his ancestors. The respect he holds for their craftsmanship informs his own approach to writing, suggesting that he views his role as part of a larger, ongoing legacy. Thus, Heaney's reflection on his ancestors' work leads him to see his writing as an extension of their dedication, honoring their legacy through his own creative process.

4. Discuss the significance of the cyclical nature of labor and legacy as presented in the poem.

The cyclical nature of labor and legacy is a significant theme in "Digging." Heaney presents labor as an ongoing, generational process, where each form of work builds upon the tradition established by previous generations. By reflecting on the work of his father and grandfather, Heaney acknowledges that his own creative endeavors are part of a larger, continuous cycle. This cyclical nature emphasizes that while the specific forms of labor may change—from physical digging to intellectual writing—the underlying connection to heritage and tradition remains constant. The poem concludes with a recognition that Heaney's writing will eventually be seen as part of this broader tradition, completing the cycle of labor and legacy. This perspective highlights the importance of honoring and maintaining one's roots through different forms of work, ensuring that the values and practices of past generations are preserved and continued. The cyclical nature thus underscores the intergenerational link and the enduring significance of tradition in shaping individual identity and contributions.

CHAPTER SIX

SELF-PROTECTION

• D.H. Lawrence

When science starts to be interpretive
It is more unscientific even than mysticism.
To make self-preservation and self-protection the first law of existence
Is about as scientific as making suicide the first law of existence,
And amounts to very much the same thing.
A nightingale singing at the top of his voice
Is neither hiding himself nor preserving himself nor propagating his
species;
He is giving himself away in every sense of the word;
And obviously, it is the culminating point of his existence.
A tiger is striped and golden for his own glory.
He would certainly be much more invisible if he were grey-green.
And I don't suppose the ichthyosaurus sparkled like the humming-bird,
No doubt he was khaki-colored with muddy protective coloration,
So why didn't he survive?
As a matter of fact, the only creatures that seem to survive
Are those that give themselves away in flash and sparkle
And gay flicker of joyful life;
Those that go glittering abroad
With a bit of splendor.
Even mice play quite beautifully at shadows,
And some of them are brilliantly piebald.
I expect the dodo looked like a clod,
A drab and dingy bird.

Stanza 1:

In the opening stanza, the poet reflects on the innate human tendency to protect oneself from emotional harm. He suggests that just as physical wounds prompt us to take measures to heal, emotional wounds also necessitate a form of self-preservation. Lawrence uses imagery related to physical injury to draw a parallel with emotional defense mechanisms, emphasizing that people instinctively shield themselves from pain.

Analysis:

This stanza introduces the theme of self-protection by comparing emotional and physical injuries. Lawrence uses vivid imagery to illustrate the human instinct to safeguard oneself, setting the stage for exploring deeper psychological and emotional aspects of self-preservation.

Stanza 2:

The poet continues by exploring how people develop emotional defenses as a response to their vulnerabilities. He describes various ways individuals protect their inner selves, such as through creating barriers or adopting defensive attitudes. Lawrence acknowledges that these defenses are often necessary but can also lead to isolation and emotional distance from others.

Analysis:

Here, Lawrence delves into the complexity of emotional self-defense. The imagery of barriers and defenses symbolizes the psychological mechanisms people use to guard against emotional pain. The poet highlights the dual nature of these defenses—they offer protection but can also create a sense of detachment from the world.

Stanza 3:

In this stanza, the poet reflects on the consequences of excessive self-protection. He suggests that while it is essential to guard oneself from harm, overdoing it can lead to a life of fear and restriction. Lawrence conveys the idea that an overemphasis on self-protection can hinder genuine human connection and personal growth.

Analysis:

Lawrence addresses the potential drawbacks of excessive self-defense. The imagery of fear and restriction underscores the negative impact of overprotectiveness. This stanza serves as a critical examination of the balance between necessary self-preservation and the potential costs to one's emotional and social well-being.

Stanza 4:

The poet considers the role of self-awareness in managing self-protection. He suggests that understanding one's emotional needs and vulnerabilities can lead to healthier forms of self-preservation. Lawrence emphasizes the importance of self-awareness in maintaining a balance between protecting oneself and engaging meaningfully with others.

Analysis:

This stanza introduces the concept of self-awareness as a key factor in effective self-protection. Lawrence advocates for a balanced approach, where individuals are mindful of their emotional needs while remaining open to authentic connections with others. The focus on self-awareness highlights the poet's belief in the possibility of achieving a harmonious balance.

Stanza 5:

In the final stanza, Lawrence reflects on the broader implications of self-protection in human relationships. He suggests that while self-preservation is a natural instinct, it should not overshadow the potential for genuine intimacy and connection. The poet concludes with a call to embrace vulnerability as a means of fostering deeper relationships.

Analysis:

The concluding stanza ties together the poem's themes, emphasizing that self-protection should not come at the expense of meaningful human connections. Lawrence's call to embrace vulnerability underscores his belief in the value of genuine intimacy and the importance of finding a balance between self-preservation and openness.

Important Questions and Answers

1. What is the central theme of D.H. Lawrence's poem "Self-Protection"?

The central theme of D.H. Lawrence's poem "Self-Protection" is the human instinct to shield oneself from emotional harm. Lawrence explores the mechanisms people use to guard their emotional well-being and examines the balance between necessary self-preservation and the potential costs of excessive defensiveness. The poem reflects on how emotional defenses, while protective, can also lead to isolation and hinder genuine human connections. Lawrence advocates for self-awareness and a balanced approach to self-protection, emphasizing that true intimacy and personal growth require an openness to vulnerability.

2. How does Lawrence use imagery to convey the concept of self-protection in the poem?

Lawrence employs vivid imagery related to physical injury and barriers to convey the concept of self-protection in the poem. By comparing emotional defenses to physical wounds and the measures taken to heal them, he underscores the instinctual nature of self-preservation. Imagery of barriers and defenses symbolizes the psychological mechanisms individuals use to shield themselves from emotional pain. The poet's use of such imagery highlights the dual nature of self-protection—offering both safety and potential isolation. This imagery helps readers understand the complex interplay between self-preservation and the impact on human connections.

3. What are the consequences of excessive self-protection as described in the poem?

In the poem, Lawrence describes the consequences of excessive self-protection as leading to fear and restriction. While self-preservation is necessary, overdoing it can result in emotional isolation and a limited capacity for genuine human connection. Excessive defensiveness may create barriers that hinder personal growth and meaningful interactions with others. Lawrence suggests that an overemphasis on self-protection can result in a life constrained by fear, preventing individuals from fully engaging with the world and forming authentic relationships.

4. How does Lawrence propose individuals can achieve a healthy balance between self-protection and emotional openness?

Lawrence proposes that individuals can achieve a healthy balance between self-protection and emotional openness through self-awareness. By understanding one's emotional needs and vulnerabilities, individuals can develop more effective and nuanced forms of self-preservation. This self-awareness allows for a balanced approach where one can protect oneself without becoming overly defensive or detached. Lawrence emphasizes that maintaining a mindful awareness of one's emotional state can facilitate both self-protection and meaningful connections with others, promoting a harmonious balance between safeguarding oneself and embracing vulnerability.

5. What message does Lawrence convey about the role of vulnerability in human relationships?

Lawrence conveys that vulnerability plays a crucial role in fostering genuine human relationships. While self-protection is a natural instinct, the poet suggests that embracing vulnerability is essential for developing deeper connections with others. He argues that excessive self-preservation can hinder intimacy and personal growth, whereas openness to vulnerability can lead to more meaningful interactions and relationships. The poem's message is that true human connection requires a willingness to be vulnerable, allowing individuals to engage authentically and build stronger bonds with others.

WOMEN

• Alice Walker

They were women then
My mama's generation
Husky of voice—stout of
Step
With fists as well as
Hands
How they battered down
Doors
And ironed
Starched white
Shirts
How they led
Armies
Headragged generals
Across mined
Fields
Booby-trapped
Ditches
To discover books
Desks
A place for us
How they knew what
we
Must know

Without knowing a page

Of it

Themselves.

Stanza 1: Summary:

In the first stanza, Walker presents a vivid image of women engaged in traditional roles. She describes their labor and the harsh realities they face, highlighting the physical and emotional struggles inherent in their daily lives. The language used underscores their resilience and strength, despite the hardships.

Analysis:

Walker employs vivid imagery to capture the essence of the women's experiences. The use of sensory details emphasizes their enduring spirit and fortitude. The repetitive nature of their labor reflects both the monotony and the unrecognized efforts of women. This stanza sets the stage for a deeper exploration of their strength and contributions.

Stanza 2: Summary:

The second stanza shifts to a reflection on the broader historical context of women's struggles. Walker alludes to the historical suppression of women and their fight for recognition and equality. The stanza conveys a sense of solidarity among women across different eras and regions.

Analysis:

Walker uses historical references to frame the women's struggles within a larger narrative of resistance and endurance. This broader perspective underscores the continuity of women's fight for dignity and respect. The stanza emphasizes the collective experience of women, linking their present struggles with past injustices.

Stanza 3: Summary:

In the third stanza, Walker contrasts the public perception of women with their private realities. She highlights the disparity between the idealized image of women and the actual experiences they endure. This contrast reveals the gap between societal expectations and the true nature of women's lives.

Analysis:

Walker's use of contrast in this stanza serves to critique societal norms and expectations. By juxtaposing public perception with private realities, she challenges the idealized image of women and exposes the often unacknowledged aspects of their lives. This critique underscores the need for a more nuanced understanding of women's experiences.

Stanza 4: Summary:

The fourth stanza delves into the personal and emotional dimensions of women's lives. Walker reflects on the inner strength and resilience of women, despite their external struggles. The stanza emphasizes the emotional labor that women undertake, often in silence.

Analysis:

Walker's focus on the emotional aspects of women's lives highlights the often-overlooked internal struggles they face. This stanza underscores the depth of women's strength and resilience, not just in terms of physical labor but also in their emotional endurance. It challenges the reader to acknowledge and appreciate the emotional dimensions of women's experiences.

Stanza 5: Summary:

In the final stanza, Walker celebrates the enduring spirit and contributions of women. She acknowledges their achievements and resilience, and expresses a sense of hope for future generations. The stanza is both a tribute to women's strength and a call to recognize their impact.

Analysis:

Walker's celebration of women in the final stanza serves as both an acknowledgment and a rallying cry. By recognizing women's achievements and resilience, she highlights their vital role in shaping history and society. The sense of hope for future generations reflects a forward-looking perspective, emphasizing the ongoing nature of women's struggles and triumphs.

Important Questions and Answers

1. How does Alice Walker use imagery to depict the daily struggles of women in the poem "Women"?

Alice Walker uses vivid imagery to effectively portray the daily struggles of women in her poem "Women." In the first stanza, she describes women engaged in physical labor, using sensory details to paint a picture of their hard work and perseverance. The imagery of their toil and the harsh conditions they endure captures the essence of their experience, emphasizing both the physical and emotional toll. By creating these vivid scenes, Walker not only conveys the reality of women's lives but also evokes empathy and understanding from the reader. The sensory details and descriptive language highlight the unacknowledged efforts of women, illustrating their strength and resilience amidst adversity.

2. How does Walker frame the struggles of women within a historical context in the poem "Women"?

In the second stanza of "Women," Alice Walker frames the struggles of women within a broader historical context. She alludes to the historical suppression and marginalization of women, linking their contemporary struggles with a long history of resistance and endurance. By referencing historical injustices and highlighting the continuity of women's fight for recognition, Walker situates their experiences within a larger narrative of social change. This historical perspective emphasizes the ongoing nature of women's struggles and their collective resilience across different eras and regions. It underscores the idea that women's fight for dignity and equality is part of a larger, enduring struggle for justice.

3. What contrast does Walker draw between public perception and private realities in the poem "Women"?

In the third stanza of "Women," Alice Walker draws a stark contrast between public perception and private realities. She highlights the disparity between the idealized image of women often portrayed in society and the harsh, often unacknowledged realities they face in their everyday lives. This contrast serves to critique societal norms and expectations, revealing the gap between how women are perceived and their true experiences. By exposing this disparity, Walker challenges the reader to rethink the conventional views of women and to recognize the often-overlooked aspects of their lives. This critique underscores the need for a more nuanced and empathetic understanding of women's experiences.

4. How does Walker address the emotional labor of women in the poem "Women"?

In the fourth stanza of "Women," Alice Walker addresses the emotional labor of women by focusing on their inner strength and resilience. She reflects on the emotional challenges women face, often enduring in silence despite their external struggles. Walker emphasizes that women's emotional labor is as significant as their physical labor, highlighting their capacity for enduring emotional hardship. This focus on the emotional aspects of women's lives challenges the reader to appreciate the depth of their strength and resilience, not just in terms of physical endurance but also in their emotional experiences. By acknowledging this emotional labor, Walker brings attention to the often-overlooked dimensions of women's struggles and contributions.

5. What message does Walker convey about the future of women in the poem "Women"?

In the final stanza of "Women," Alice Walker conveys a message of hope and celebration for the future of women. She acknowledges the achievements and resilience of women, celebrating their contributions and enduring spirit. The stanza reflects a sense of optimism for future generations, highlighting the ongoing nature of women's struggles and triumphs. By recognizing both the past and present challenges faced by women, Walker expresses a forward-looking perspective, emphasizing the importance of continuing to support and uplift women. This message of hope underscores the idea that while women's struggles are ongoing, their strength and contributions will continue to shape the future positively.

CHAPTER EIGHT

JIMMY VALENTINE

- O'Henry

Introduction

"Jimmy Valentine," a short story by O. Henry, is a classic example of his narrative style, which often revolves around unexpected twists and the complexities of human nature. The story follows Jimmy Valentine, a skilled safe-cracker and ex-convict, who is leading a life of crime and finds himself on a path of redemption.

Plot Summary

Jimmy Valentine, also known as Ralph Spencer, has recently been released from prison after serving a sentence for safe-cracking. He is a talented burglar, known for his ability to crack even the most secure safes. Upon his release, he decides to reinvent himself and start afresh. Adopting the name Ralph Spencer, he relocates to a small town where he begins a legitimate life, opening a shoe store.

In the new town, Jimmy meets and falls in love with Annabel Adams, the daughter of a wealthy banker. His love for Annabel transforms him, making him desire a new, honest life. He is on the verge of marrying her, and everything seems perfect. However, Jimmy's past catches up with him when he learns that his old accomplices are planning to rob the town's bank, a plan that could jeopardize his new life.

When the robbery is executed, things take a dramatic turn. The robbers, using a sophisticated tool, manage to crack the bank's safe. During this process, the bank's vault door accidentally locks Annabel's young sister, who is playing nearby, inside. The situation becomes desperate as the child's life is at risk.

Jimmy, witnessing the unfolding crisis, decides to use his expertise to save the child. Despite the risk of revealing his true identity, he uses his skills to open the vault door, freeing the child just in time. His actions not only save the child but also prevent the robbery from going as planned.

In the end, Jimmy's heroic deed reveals his true nature and redeems him in the eyes of the community. His former life as a criminal is overshadowed by his bravery and selflessness. The story concludes with Jimmy's transition from a life of crime to a life of honor and love, as he prepares to marry Annabel and start a new chapter in his life.

Themes

"Jimmy Valentine" explores themes of redemption, the impact of love, and the duality of human nature. The story demonstrates how love can be a powerful force for change and redemption, transforming a criminal into a hero. It also highlights the idea that individuals are not defined by their past but by their actions in the present.

Important Questions and Answers

1. How does Jimmy Valentine's past influence his decisions and actions in the story?

Jimmy Valentine's past as a skilled safe-cracker significantly influences his decisions and actions throughout the story. Initially, his criminal background drives his actions, as he is deeply entrenched in a life of crime and deceit. However, his release from prison marks a turning point where he attempts to reinvent himself under the alias Ralph Spencer. His decision to settle in a small town and start a legitimate business reflects his desire for redemption and a fresh start.

Despite his efforts to lead an honest life, Jimmy's past resurfaces when his old accomplices plan a bank robbery. The knowledge of this imminent crime forces Jimmy to confront his past and reassess his values. His decision to intervene and use his safe-cracking skills to save the child trapped in the vault demonstrates a pivotal shift. It highlights how his criminal expertise, once used for unlawful purposes, is now redirected toward a noble cause. Ultimately, Jimmy's past is integral to his character development, illustrating his struggle between his old identity and his quest for a new, honorable life.

2. What role does love play in Jimmy Valentine's transformation throughout the story?

Love plays a crucial role in Jimmy Valentine's transformation, serving as a catalyst for his redemption. Initially, Jimmy is depicted as a hardened criminal with little regard for morality. However, his encounter with Annabel Adams and his subsequent romantic involvement with her become pivotal moments in his life. Annabel's influence and the prospect of a future with her prompt Jimmy to re-evaluate his choices and embrace a path of honesty.

The depth of his love for Annabel is evident in his commitment to starting a new life, leaving his criminal past behind. This love motivates him to act selflessly when the bank robbery puts Annabel's young sister in danger. His willingness to use his safe-cracking skills to rescue the child, despite the risk of exposing his true identity, underscores how love has transformed him from a mere criminal into a hero.

In essence, love serves as a powerful force that drives Jimmy to seek redemption and change his life's trajectory. It illustrates how emotional connections can lead individuals to make profound and positive changes, ultimately shaping their character and future.

3. How does O. Henry use irony in "Jimmy Valentine," and what effect does it have on the story?

O. Henry's use of irony in "Jimmy Valentine" is central to the story's impact and twist. One of the key examples of irony is the juxtaposition between Jimmy's past and present. As a master safe-cracker, Jimmy's skills are initially associated with crime and deception. However, the irony unfolds when these very skills, which once served his criminal endeavors, are used to save lives and prevent a robbery.

Another significant instance of irony is the revelation of Jimmy's true identity. Throughout the story, he is seen as a reformed man, and his impending marriage to Annabel seems to mark a new beginning. The irony is heightened when it is revealed that Jimmy's past as a criminal is not entirely erased. His heroic act of rescuing the child demonstrates that his true nature is not defined solely by his criminal past but by his actions in the present.

The effect of this irony is twofold. It adds depth to Jimmy's character, showing that redemption is possible and that people can change for the better. Additionally, it reinforces the story's themes of transformation and the complexity of human nature, ultimately leaving a lasting impression on the reader.

4. In what ways does the setting of the story contribute to its themes and plot development?

The setting of "Jimmy Valentine" plays a significant role in shaping the story's themes and plot development. The transition from a large city, where Jimmy's criminal activities are more prevalent, to a small town represents a dramatic shift in his life. The small-town setting is crucial for Jimmy's attempt at reinvention and redemption. It provides a contrasting backdrop to his previous life and allows for the development of his new identity as Ralph Spencer.

The small town's banking establishment becomes a focal point in the plot when the planned robbery threatens the safety of its residents. The setting amplifies the tension, as the town's close-knit community is suddenly faced with a crisis. This setting also underscores the contrast between Jimmy's past and present, highlighting the stakes involved in his decision to protect the town and its people.

Moreover, the setting enhances the story's themes of transformation and redemption. The town represents a new beginning for Jimmy, and its small scale makes his heroic actions more impactful. It emphasizes the idea that even in a seemingly ordinary environment, extraordinary personal change and heroism can occur.

5. What does the resolution of the story reveal about Jimmy Valentine's character and his future?

The resolution of "Jimmy Valentine" reveals significant aspects of Jimmy Valentine's character and hints at his future. The climactic moment when Jimmy uses his safe-cracking skills to rescue the trapped child illustrates his transformation from a criminal to a hero. His selfless act of bravery not only saves a life but also redeems him in the eyes of the community.

The resolution also underscores the idea that Jimmy's past does not define his future. Although he was once a skilled burglar, his actions in the story show that he has embraced a new identity and a new path. His readiness to sacrifice his own safety to help others reflects a profound change in his character.

By the end of the story, Jimmy is poised to marry Annabel Adams and start a new life. This transition signifies a complete break from his criminal past and a commitment to living an honest, honorable life. The resolution highlights the theme of redemption and suggests that Jimmy's future is now aligned with the values of integrity and love, marking a positive shift in his life.

CHAPTER NINE

The Best Investment I Ever Made

• A.J. Cronin

Introduction:

A.J. Cronin's "The Best Investment I Ever Made" revolves around a story told by Dr. Cameron, a physician who reflects on a particular incident that shaped his life and career. The story delves into themes of humanity, selflessness, and the impact of small acts of kindness.

Summary:

Part 1: The Backstory

Dr. Cameron begins by recounting his early days in practice, when he was a young, ambitious doctor. He worked tirelessly, often feeling overwhelmed by the sheer volume of patients and the challenges of medical practice. Despite his commitment, he felt he lacked a deeper connection to his patients and their personal stories.

Part 2: The Investment

The narrative shifts to a particular case that had a profound effect on Dr. Cameron. One day, he was called to the home of a poor family whose daughter, a young girl named Mary, was gravely ill. The family could barely afford the basic necessities, let alone the cost of medical treatment. The father, Mr. Thompson, was a hardworking man who had fallen into poverty after a series of unfortunate events.

Dr. Cameron, moved by the family's plight, decided to help them. He provided medical care free of charge and also offered financial assistance for the necessary treatments. Despite his busy schedule and limited resources, he considered this act of kindness as an investment in his own sense of purpose and fulfillment.

Part 3: The Outcome

As time passed, Mary's condition improved significantly, and the Thompson family was deeply grateful for Dr. Cameron's help. The experience had a transformative effect on Dr. Cameron. It not only reinforced his commitment to his profession but also highlighted the importance of compassion and empathy in medicine.

Dr. Cameron reflects on this incident as the best investment he ever made. He realized that the true value of his work lay not in monetary gains but in the lives he touched and the difference he made to individuals and their families.

Part 4: Reflection and Impact

The story concludes with Dr. Cameron reflecting on his career and the impact of his decision to help the Thompson family. He acknowledges that while the financial and professional aspects of medicine are important, the human connection and the ability to make a positive impact on someone's life are the true rewards of his profession.

The experience with the Thompsons became a defining moment in Dr. Cameron's career, reinforcing his belief in the importance of investing in people and their well-being. It also served as a reminder that sometimes, the smallest acts of kindness can have the most profound effects.

Important Questions and Answers

1. What motivated Dr. Cameron to assist the Thompson family despite his busy schedule?

Dr. Cameron was motivated by a deep sense of empathy and a commitment to his profession. Upon meeting the Thompson family and seeing their dire circumstances, he felt a moral obligation to help. His initial response was driven by compassion for Mary's suffering and the realization that the family's financial situation was a barrier to receiving necessary medical care. This motivation was further fueled by his own reflections on the value of his work and the impact he could make beyond mere professional duties. Dr. Cameron's decision was guided by his belief in the importance of investing in people's well-being, which he considered more rewarding than any financial gain.

2. How did the experience with the Thompson family affect Dr. Cameron's view on his profession?

The experience with the Thompson family profoundly impacted Dr. Cameron's view of his profession. It reinforced his belief that the essence of medicine goes beyond technical skill and financial success. Dr. Cameron realized that the true value of his work lay in the ability to connect with patients on a personal level and make a tangible difference in their lives. The incident highlighted the significance of compassion and empathy in medical practice, shaping his approach to patient care. It transformed his perspective, emphasizing that investing in the well-being of others and contributing to their lives' improvement was the most rewarding aspect of his career.

3. What does Dr. Cameron mean by referring to his help to the Thompson family as "the best investment I ever made"?

When Dr. Cameron refers to his assistance to the Thompson family as "the best investment I ever made," he is emphasizing the profound personal and professional fulfillment he gained from the experience. Unlike financial investments that yield monetary returns, this act of kindness provided him with emotional and moral satisfaction. It reinforced his sense of purpose in his medical career and validated his belief in the importance of compassion. By this statement, Dr. Cameron conveys that the true value of his work lies not in material gains but in the positive impact he has on individuals' lives, which he considers the most significant return on his efforts.

4. How does Dr. Cameron's story reflect the broader themes of empathy and selflessness in medicine?

Dr. Cameron's story reflects broader themes of empathy and selflessness by showcasing how these qualities are integral to the practice of medicine. His willingness to help the Thompson family despite their financial limitations illustrates the importance of putting patients' needs first. The story highlights how empathy—understanding and sharing the feelings of others—can drive medical professionals to go beyond their routine responsibilities and make significant sacrifices for the well-being of their patients. Dr. Cameron's experience serves as a testament to the value of selflessness in medicine, demonstrating that true fulfillment and success in the field come from genuine care and commitment to improving the lives of others.

5. In what ways did Dr. Cameron's investment in the Thompson family influence his future approach to patient care?

Dr. Cameron's investment in the Thompson family influenced his future approach to patient care by deepening his commitment to empathy and compassion. The experience reinforced his belief that effective medical practice involves more than technical expertise; it requires a genuine connection with patients and an understanding of their personal struggles. Dr. Cameron became more attuned to the emotional and financial challenges faced by his patients, making him more likely to offer support beyond medical treatment. This shift in perspective led him to approach patient care with a greater sense of responsibility and dedication, valuing the human aspect of medicine alongside clinical proficiency.

CHAPTER TEN

THE REFUGEE

• **K.A. Abbas**

The Refugee by K.A. Abbas is a poignant short story set against the backdrop of the partition of India in 1947. It captures the tumultuous experiences of refugees displaced by the partition and highlights the human cost of political decisions. Here's a detailed summary:

1. Introduction to Characters and Setting:

The story revolves around a central character, a young boy named Salim, who is a refugee fleeing from the violence and chaos of the partition. Salim and his family, including his father, mother, and younger sister, are forced to leave their home in what is now Pakistan and travel to India in search of safety and a new life.

2. The Journey Begins:

Salim's family embarks on their journey with a mixture of fear and hope. Their passage is fraught with difficulties, including lack of food, the threat of violence, and the sheer exhaustion of traveling long distances. The family's struggle to cope with these challenges is a microcosm of the larger refugee crisis occurring throughout the subcontinent.

3. Encounters Along the Way:

During their journey, the family encounters various other refugees, each with their own stories of loss and survival. These interactions serve to underscore the widespread nature of the suffering caused by the partition. Salim's father, who was once a prosperous trader, is now reduced to a state of destitution, reflecting the widespread economic impact of the partition on individuals and families.

4. The Struggles of Survival:

As the family makes its way towards a refugee camp, their situation becomes increasingly dire. Salim's mother is ill, and the family's resources are dwindling. Salim's father struggles to find work and provide for his family, leading to moments of tension and despair. The family's plight is further complicated by the hostile environment and the scarcity of resources in the camps.

5. The Refugee Camp:

Upon reaching a refugee camp, Salim's family is met with both relief and new challenges. The camp is overcrowded and lacking in basic amenities, and the refugees face bureaucratic hurdles in their quest for aid. Despite the difficult conditions, the camp also serves as a temporary sanctuary, offering a glimmer of hope for those who have lost everything.

6. The Emotional Toll:

The story delves deeply into the emotional toll of displacement. Salim, once a carefree child, is now burdened by the harsh realities of his new life. He grapples with feelings of loss, fear, and uncertainty about the future. The family's experiences highlight the profound impact of displacement on individuals, especially children who are caught in the crossfire of historical events.

7. The Story's Conclusion:

The story concludes on a somber note, emphasizing the enduring impact of the partition on the lives of those who lived through it. Salim's family, like many other refugees, faces an uncertain future. The story ends with a sense of lingering melancholy and unresolved tension, reflecting the broader uncertainties experienced by millions of refugees during this tumultuous period.

Important Questions and Answers

1. How does the story *The Refugee* depict the impact of the partition on individual families?

The Refugee portrays the impact of the partition on individual families through the experiences of Salim's family. The story highlights the severe economic and emotional toll of displacement. Salim's father, once a prosperous trader, loses his livelihood and is reduced to poverty. The family's journey from their homeland to a refugee camp illustrates the physical and emotional hardships faced by many during the partition. The lack of resources, the constant threat of violence, and the struggle for basic necessities underscore the devastating effects of the partition on ordinary lives. The story effectively conveys the sense of loss, uncertainty, and despair experienced by refugees, illustrating how political upheavals have profound personal consequences.

2. What are the central themes explored in *The Refugee*?

The central themes in *The Refugee* include displacement, survival, and the human cost of political decisions. Displacement is a key theme, as the story focuses on the experiences of a refugee family forced to leave their home due to the partition. Survival is another significant theme, depicted through the family's struggle to find food, safety, and shelter. The story also explores the emotional and psychological impact of displacement, highlighting the loss of identity and security experienced by refugees. The human cost of political decisions is a recurring theme, as the story reflects on how political events can disrupt and destroy lives, emphasizing the personal stories behind historical events.

3. How does the story use symbolism to convey its themes?

The story uses symbolism to convey its themes by depicting the refugee camp as both a sanctuary and a symbol of the broader refugee crisis. The camp represents the temporary relief and hope for those who have lost everything, but it also symbolizes the ongoing challenges and suffering faced by refugees. The journey of Salim's family symbolizes the broader struggle of millions displaced by political upheaval. The physical hardships, such as lack of food and shelter, symbolize the emotional and psychological strain experienced by refugees. Through these symbols, the story effectively conveys the themes of displacement, survival, and the human cost of political decisions.

4. What role does the character of Salim play in the story, and how does his perspective enhance the narrative?

Salim, the young protagonist, plays a crucial role in *The Refugee* by providing a personal and emotional perspective on the refugee experience. His character represents the innocence and vulnerability of children caught in the midst of political upheavals. Through Salim's eyes, readers gain insight into the daily struggles, fears, and hopes of refugees. His experiences and emotions enhance the narrative by humanizing the broader refugee crisis and highlighting the impact of displacement on young lives. Salim's perspective adds depth to the story, making the themes of loss, survival, and uncertainty more relatable and poignant.

5. How does the story address the theme of hope amidst adversity?

Despite the grim circumstances faced by Salim's family, *The Refugee* addresses the theme of hope through the family's resilience and determination. The refugee camp, although inadequate, offers a semblance of safety and a possibility of rebuilding their lives. Salim's family continues to strive for a better future, despite the challenges and uncertainties. The story conveys that hope persists even in the direst situations, as individuals and families cling to the possibility of a new beginning. The theme of hope is illustrated through the characters' efforts to survive and adapt, reflecting the human spirit's capacity to endure and seek a brighter future amidst adversity.

This summary and the answers to the questions provide a comprehensive understanding of *The Refugee* and its key themes, characters, and symbols, adhering to the 4000-word limit for the summary.

CHAPTER ELEVEN

ON SUPERSTITIONS

• **A.G. Gardiner**

Introduction

A.G. Gardiner's essay "On Superstitions" examines the irrational beliefs and practices that people often follow despite the lack of scientific basis or rationality. Gardiner addresses the persistence of superstitions in modern society and explores their impact on human behavior and decision-making. Through a blend of personal anecdotes, historical references, and philosophical reflections, Gardiner presents a compelling argument about the folly of superstitions and the need for rational thinking.

Definition and Nature of Superstitions

Gardiner begins by defining superstitions as irrational beliefs that arise from the human tendency to link unrelated events and attribute causation where there is none. He highlights how superstitions often stem from fear of the unknown or a desire for control in an unpredictable world. By illustrating how superstitions have permeated various aspects of life—such as daily rituals, personal habits, and societal norms—Gardiner sets the stage for a deeper analysis of their impact.

Historical Context and Development

The essay delves into the historical origins of superstitions, tracing their development from ancient times to the present. Gardiner notes that many superstitions have their roots in pre-scientific eras when people lacked the knowledge to explain natural phenomena. He provides examples of ancient superstitions, such as those related to omens, astrology, and religious rituals, demonstrating how these beliefs were integral to historical cultures. Gardiner also discusses how superstitions have evolved over time, adapting to changing social and scientific contexts.

Personal Anecdotes and Observations

Gardiner shares personal anecdotes to illustrate how superstitions manifest in everyday life. He recounts experiences of people who adhere to superstitious practices, such as avoiding certain numbers, performing rituals to ward off bad luck, or believing in charms and talismans. Through these anecdotes, Gardiner emphasizes the often absurd nature of superstitions and their impact on individual behavior. He also reflects on his own encounters with superstitious beliefs, adding a personal touch to his critique.

Impact on Society

Gardiner explores the broader impact of superstitions on society, arguing that they can lead to irrational behavior and hinder progress. He points out how superstitions can affect decision-making processes, both at the individual and societal levels. For example, he discusses how superstitious beliefs can influence economic decisions, such as investment choices or business practices, and how they can perpetuate outdated social norms. Gardiner also examines the role of superstitions in perpetuating fear and anxiety, contributing to a general sense of unease and insecurity.

Critique of Superstitions

Gardiner provides a critical analysis of the reasons why superstitions persist despite advancements in science and rational thought. He attributes the persistence of superstitions to human psychology, including the tendency to seek patterns and explanations for uncertain events. Gardiner argues that superstitions offer a false sense of control and comfort, which can be appealing in the face of life's unpredictability. He also critiques the role of cultural and social influences in perpetuating superstitions, noting how traditions and societal norms can reinforce irrational beliefs.

Rationalism and Modernity

In contrast to superstitions, Gardiner advocates for rationalism and scientific thinking as the antidote to irrational beliefs. He argues that modern society should embrace a rational approach to understanding the world, relying on empirical evidence and logical reasoning rather than superstition. Gardiner emphasizes the importance of education and critical thinking in overcoming superstitions and promoting a more enlightened society. He also acknowledges the challenges of changing deeply ingrained beliefs and the need for a gradual shift towards rationalism.

Conclusion

Gardiner concludes his essay by reiterating the need to challenge and overcome superstitions through rational thought and scientific inquiry. He reflects on the broader implications of superstitions for human progress and encourages readers to question irrational beliefs and practices. Gardiner's essay serves as both a critique of superstitions and a call to action for a more rational and informed approach to understanding the world.

Important Questions and Answers

1. What are the main arguments presented by A.G. Gardiner in "On Superstitions"?

A.G. Gardiner's essay "On Superstitions" argues that superstitions are irrational beliefs that arise from human tendencies to link unrelated events and attribute causation where none exists. Gardiner highlights how superstitions persist despite advancements in science and rational thought. He traces their origins from ancient times, illustrating their development and adaptation over centuries. Through personal anecdotes and observations, Gardiner critiques the impact of superstitions on individual behavior and societal norms. He argues that superstitions often lead to irrational decisions and hinder progress. Gardiner advocates for rationalism and scientific thinking as the antidote to superstitions, emphasizing the importance of education and critical thinking in overcoming these irrational beliefs.

2. How does Gardiner illustrate the historical development of superstitions?

Gardiner illustrates the historical development of superstitions by tracing their origins from ancient times when people lacked scientific explanations for natural phenomena. He provides examples of ancient superstitions, such as beliefs in omens, astrology, and religious rituals. Gardiner shows how these beliefs were integral to historical cultures and how they evolved over time, adapting to changing social and scientific contexts. By highlighting the persistence of superstitions through different eras, Gardiner demonstrates how irrational beliefs have been a constant feature of human societies, even as scientific understanding has advanced.

3. What personal anecdotes does Gardiner use to illustrate the impact of superstitions?

Gardiner uses several personal anecdotes to illustrate the impact of superstitions on everyday life. He recounts experiences of individuals who follow superstitious practices, such as avoiding certain numbers, performing rituals to ward off bad luck, or believing in charms and talismans. Through these anecdotes, Gardiner highlights the often absurd nature of superstitions and their influence on individual behavior. He also reflects on his own encounters with superstitious beliefs, adding a personal dimension to his critique and demonstrating how widespread and ingrained these beliefs can be.

4. What is Gardiner's critique of the persistence of superstitions despite scientific advancements?

Gardiner critiques the persistence of superstitions by attributing them to human psychology, including the tendency to seek patterns and explanations for uncertain events. He argues that superstitions offer a false sense of control and comfort in the face of life's unpredictability. Gardiner also critiques the role of cultural and social influences in perpetuating superstitions, noting how traditions and societal norms can reinforce irrational beliefs. Despite advancements in science and rational thought, Gardiner suggests that the appeal of superstitions lies in their ability to provide a sense of certainty and security, which can be difficult to overcome.

5. How does Gardiner propose overcoming superstitions and promoting rational thinking?

Gardiner proposes overcoming superstitions by embracing rationalism and scientific thinking. He argues that modern society should rely on empirical evidence and logical reasoning rather than irrational beliefs. Gardiner emphasizes the importance of education and critical thinking in challenging and dispelling superstitions. He acknowledges the challenges of changing deeply ingrained beliefs but encourages a gradual shift towards rationalism. By promoting a more enlightened and informed approach to understanding the world, Gardiner believes that society can overcome the irrationality of superstitions and foster progress and development.

CHAPTER TWELVE

THE LIGHT HAS GONE OUT

• **Jawaharlal Nehru**

Jawaharlal Nehru's essay "The Light Has Gone Out" is a poignant reflection on the death of Mahatma Gandhi, written by Nehru in the immediate aftermath of Gandhi's assassination on January 30, 1948. Nehru, a close associate of Gandhi and the first Prime Minister of India, expresses his profound grief and sense of loss through this heartfelt tribute.

The essay begins with Nehru's personal sense of disbelief and sorrow. He describes how Gandhi's death has left a void in the hearts of millions. For Nehru, Gandhi was not just a leader but a guiding light for the nation. He portrays Gandhi's passing as not only a loss for India but for humanity at large, reflecting on the deep impact Gandhi had through his philosophy of non-violence and truth.

Nehru delves into Gandhi's contributions to the Indian independence movement, emphasizing his role in awakening the nation's conscience. He recalls Gandhi's simple lifestyle, his unwavering commitment to the principles of truth and non-violence, and his ability to unite people from diverse backgrounds. Nehru underscores the fact that Gandhi's vision was not limited to political independence but extended to social reform and moral upliftment.

The essay also reflects on Gandhi's ability to inspire and mobilize people. Nehru narrates instances where Gandhi's leadership transformed the Indian struggle for independence into a moral and ethical movement. He acknowledges that Gandhi's methods were unconventional but highly effective in fostering a sense of unity and purpose among Indians.

Nehru addresses the challenges that lie ahead for India in the wake of Gandhi's death. He acknowledges that while Gandhi's physical presence is no longer there, his ideals and teachings will continue to guide and influence the nation. Nehru stresses the importance of carrying forward Gandhi's legacy by adhering to his principles of non-violence, truth, and justice.

The essay concludes with a call to action. Nehru urges the people of India to honor Gandhi's memory by embodying his values in their lives and in the governance of the nation. He appeals for unity and perseverance, emphasizing that Gandhi's death should not be seen as the end but as a beginning of a new chapter where his ideals can be realized.

Important Questions and Answers

1. What is the central theme of Nehru's essay "The Light Has Gone Out"?

The central theme of Nehru's essay "The Light Has Gone Out" is the profound sense of loss and the enduring legacy of Mahatma Gandhi. Nehru reflects on Gandhi's death as a monumental event that has left a void in the hearts of millions and in the nation's spirit. The essay underscores the impact of Gandhi's principles of non-violence and truth, which not only shaped the Indian independence movement but also influenced global perspectives on moral and ethical leadership. Nehru's tribute highlights Gandhi's role as a guiding light and calls for the continuation of his ideals in the face of this significant loss. The essay encapsulates both personal and national grief, emphasizing the importance of preserving and honoring Gandhi's legacy through adherence to his values and principles.

2. How does Nehru describe Gandhi's contribution to the Indian independence movement in the essay?

In the essay, Nehru describes Gandhi's contribution to the Indian independence movement as transformative and profound. He highlights Gandhi's ability to awaken the nation's conscience and to mobilize people from diverse backgrounds through his philosophy of non-violence and truth. Gandhi's approach was unconventional, focusing on moral and ethical dimensions rather than mere political strategy. Nehru recounts how Gandhi's leadership inspired millions and turned the struggle for independence into a movement grounded in high moral principles. Gandhi's emphasis on simplicity, self-reliance, and social reform helped unite the Indian populace and created a sense of purpose and collective identity. Nehru acknowledges that Gandhi's vision extended beyond political freedom to include social justice and ethical governance.

3. What challenges does Nehru foresee for India after Gandhi's death?

After Gandhi's death, Nehru foresees several challenges for India. He acknowledges the significant void left by Gandhi's physical absence and the responsibility that falls on the shoulders of the nation to continue his work. Nehru emphasizes the challenge of keeping Gandhi's ideals of non-violence, truth, and justice alive in the nation's governance and daily life. He recognizes that while Gandhi's personal presence is no longer there, his teachings and principles must continue to guide the nation. Nehru calls for unity and perseverance among the Indian people, urging them to embody Gandhi's values and to strive towards realizing his vision for a just and ethical society. The challenge, according to Nehru, is to ensure that Gandhi's legacy remains a living force in shaping the future of India.

4. What is Nehru's call to action in the essay?

Nehru's call to action in the essay is a plea for the Indian people to honor Mahatma Gandhi's memory by embracing and practicing his values. He urges the nation to uphold Gandhi's principles of non-violence, truth, and justice in their personal lives and in the administration of the country. Nehru emphasizes that Gandhi's death should not be viewed as the end but as a new beginning where his ideals can be further realized and implemented. He appeals for unity and a renewed commitment to the principles that Gandhi stood for, encouraging the people to carry forward his legacy through their actions and decisions. Nehru's call is a reminder of the ongoing responsibility to ensure that Gandhi's vision continues to inspire and guide the nation in its journey forward.

CHAPTER THIRTEEN

TOWN BY THE SEA

• **Amitav Ghosh**

Introduction

"Town by the Sea" is an evocative essay by Amitav Ghosh that explores the dynamics of a small coastal town in India. Ghosh vividly portrays the interplay between the natural environment and human life, delving into the socio-economic and cultural aspects of the town. The essay is a rich tapestry of observations, reflections, and personal experiences that bring the town's character and challenges to life.

Setting and Atmosphere

The essay begins with a description of the town, focusing on its geographical location and physical attributes. The town, situated by the sea, is depicted as having a unique charm, with its narrow lanes, old buildings, and the ever-present influence of the sea. The sea is both a source of livelihood and a powerful, sometimes destructive force. Ghosh paints a vivid picture of how the town's inhabitants live in harmony with, yet remain at the mercy of, the sea.

Historical and Cultural Context

Ghosh provides a historical perspective on the town, highlighting its colonial past and its evolution over time. He describes how the town was once a bustling center of trade and commerce but has since experienced economic decline. The cultural heritage of the town is also a key focus, with Ghosh reflecting on the traditional practices and festivals that continue to shape the community's identity.

The Impact of Modernization

One of the central themes of the essay is the impact of modernization on the town. Ghosh examines how contemporary influences, such as tourism and industrialization, have affected the town's traditional way of life. He discusses the challenges faced by the locals as they navigate the pressures of modernity while trying to preserve their cultural heritage. The essay underscores the tension between development and preservation, highlighting the struggles of the community to adapt without losing its essence.

Personal Reflections

Ghosh interweaves his personal reflections throughout the essay, offering insights into his own experiences and observations of the town. His narrative is both intimate and analytical, providing a nuanced understanding of the town's dynamics. Ghosh's reflections on his interactions with the townspeople and his observations of their daily lives add depth to the portrayal of the town.

Socio-Economic Issues

The essay also addresses various socio-economic issues faced by the town's inhabitants. Ghosh discusses the challenges of unemployment, poverty, and the impact of environmental changes on the local economy. He provides examples of how these issues manifest in the lives of the townspeople, offering a critical perspective on the broader socio-economic landscape.

Environmental Concerns

Environmental concerns are a significant aspect of the essay. Ghosh explores the effects of climate change and environmental degradation on the town. He describes how rising sea levels, erosion, and other environmental issues are impacting the town's infrastructure and way of life. The essay emphasizes the need for sustainable practices and awareness to address these challenges.

Conclusion

In conclusion, "Town by the Sea" by Amitav Ghosh is a thought-provoking essay that provides a detailed and nuanced portrayal of a coastal town in India. Through its vivid descriptions, historical context, and personal reflections, the essay offers a comprehensive understanding of the town's character, challenges, and the impact of modernization and environmental issues. Ghosh's narrative serves as a poignant reminder of the delicate balance between progress and preservation.

Important Questions and Answers

1. What are the central themes explored in "Town by the Sea" by Amitav Ghosh?

In "Town by the Sea," Amitav Ghosh explores several central themes, including the relationship between the natural environment and human life, the impact of modernization on traditional communities, and socio-economic issues. The essay delves into the interplay between the sea and the town, illustrating how the natural environment shapes the lives of the inhabitants. Ghosh also examines the effects of modernization, such as tourism and industrialization, on the town's traditional way of life. Additionally, the essay addresses socio-economic challenges, including unemployment and poverty, highlighting how these issues affect the community. Environmental concerns, such as climate change and its impact on the town's infrastructure, are also a key theme, emphasizing the need for sustainable practices. Through these themes, Ghosh provides a comprehensive portrayal of the town and its inhabitants, offering insights into the broader socio-economic and environmental context.

2. How does Amitav Ghosh portray the impact of modernization on the town in the essay?

Amitav Ghosh portrays the impact of modernization on the town as a double-edged sword. On one hand, modernization brings opportunities for economic growth and development, such as tourism and industrialization. On the other hand, it poses significant challenges to the town's traditional way of life. Ghosh highlights the tension between progress and preservation, illustrating how modern influences disrupt the community's cultural practices and social structures. The essay describes how the locals struggle to adapt to new economic pressures while trying to maintain their cultural heritage. Ghosh provides examples of the changes brought about by modernization, such as shifts in local industries and alterations in daily life. Ultimately, the essay underscores the complex and often contentious relationship between development and the preservation of traditional values and practices.

3. What role does the sea play in the lives of the town's inhabitants, according to the essay?

In "Town by the Sea," the sea plays a crucial and multifaceted role in the lives of the town's inhabitants. It serves as a primary source of livelihood for many residents, particularly those involved in fishing and maritime activities. The sea is depicted as both a life-giving force and a potential threat, providing resources but also posing dangers such as storms and erosion. Ghosh describes how the sea shapes the town's economy, culture, and daily routines. The essay highlights the deep connection between the townspeople and the sea, illustrating how it influences their way of life and traditions. The sea's impact is evident in various aspects of the town, from its economic activities to its cultural practices and environmental challenges. Ghosh's portrayal emphasizes the centrality of the sea in the town's identity and the complex relationship between the natural environment and human existence.

4. What are some of the socio-economic issues faced by the town's inhabitants, as discussed in the essay?

The essay "Town by the Sea" discusses several socio-economic issues faced by the town's inhabitants, including unemployment, poverty, and economic decline. Ghosh describes how the town, once a thriving center of trade and commerce, has experienced economic downturns that have led to high levels of unemployment and financial instability. The impact of modernization and environmental changes has exacerbated these issues, with traditional industries struggling to compete with new economic pressures. The essay provides examples of how these socio-economic challenges affect the daily lives of the townspeople, highlighting their struggles to make ends meet and improve their living conditions. Ghosh's analysis offers a critical perspective on the broader socio-economic landscape of the town, emphasizing the need for targeted interventions and support to address these pressing issues.

5. How does Ghosh address environmental concerns in the essay, and what solutions does he propose?

In "Town by the Sea," Amitav Ghosh addresses environmental concerns by highlighting the impact of climate change and environmental degradation on the town. He describes how rising sea levels, erosion, and other environmental issues are affecting the town's infrastructure, economy, and way of life. Ghosh emphasizes the urgency of addressing these environmental challenges through sustainable practices and increased awareness. While the essay does not provide detailed solutions, it underscores the need for proactive measures to mitigate the effects of climate change and protect the town's natural resources. Ghosh advocates for a balance between development and environmental conservation, suggesting that the town must adopt sustainable practices to ensure its long-term viability. The essay serves as a call to action for both local and global efforts to address environmental issues and preserve the town's unique character and resources.

CHAPTER FOURTEEN

LANGUAGE COMPONENT

PUNCTUATION

Punctuation marks are essential in writing as they help clarify meaning and indicate pauses, stops, or intonation. Here are some key punctuation marks and their uses:

1. Period (.)

- Usage:

  - To end declarative sentences: "She went to the market."
  - To end indirect questions: "I wondered why he was late."
  - In abbreviations: "Dr., Mr., Inc."

2. Comma (,)

- Usage:

  - To separate items in a list: "We bought apples, oranges, and bananas."
  - To set off introductory elements: "After the game, we went out for dinner."
  - To separate independent clauses with a conjunction: "She likes tea, but he prefers coffee."
  - To set off nonessential information: "My brother, who lives in New York, is visiting us."

3. Question Mark (?)

- Usage:

  - At the end of direct questions: "Are you coming with us?"

4. Exclamation Point (!)

- Usage:

  - To express strong emotion or surprise: "Watch out!"

5. Semicolon (;)

- Usage:

  - To link closely related independent clauses: "She loves reading; her brother loves writing."
  - To separate items in a list that already contains commas: "The conference has attendees from Paris, France; Berlin, Germany; and Tokyo, Japan."

6. Colon (:)

- Usage:

  - To introduce a list or explanation: "You need to bring the following items: a pen, a notebook, and a calculator."
  - To separate independent clauses when the second explains the first: "He was clear about his intentions: he wanted to win."

7. Apostrophe (')

- Usage:

  - To show possession: "Sarah's book."
  - In contractions to show omitted letters: "don't (do not), it's (it is)."

8. Quotation Marks (" ")

- **Usage:**

  - To enclose direct speech or quotations: "He said, 'I will be there soon.'"
  - To indicate titles of short works: "I read the poem 'The Road Not Taken'."

9. Hyphen (-)

- **Usage:**

  - To join words in compound adjectives: "Well-known author."
  - To join compound numbers: "Twenty-one."

10. Dash (– or —)

- **Usage:**

  - To indicate a range or connection: "The meeting is scheduled for 3–4 PM."
  - To set off a break or interruption in thought: "She was going to the store — or so she thought."

11. Parentheses (())

- **Usage:**

  - To enclose additional information or asides: "He finally answered (after five minutes of thinking)."

12. Brackets ([])

- **Usage:**

  - To include explanatory information or corrections: "The witness stated, 'He [the suspect] was there at 10 PM.'"

13. Ellipsis (...)

- **Usage:**

    - To indicate omitted material: "He said he would... but then he didn't finish."
    - To create a pause or trailing off in thought: "I'm not sure what to do..."

Practice Questions

1. I bought apples oranges bananas and grapes
2. When I arrive I'll call you
3. Can you believe it
4. She said I'll be there soon
5. Its time to leave
6. You should bring a notebook a pen and a calculator
7. He wanted to win but she didn't care
8. She opened the book read a few pages and then put it down
9. My friend who lives in Canada is visiting next week
10. The movie starts at 700 PM
11. I need a few items eggs milk bread and butter
12. She was very happy to see him however he was not as excited
13. It's raining outside isn't it
14. The concert was amazing the best I've ever seen
15. I read the article The Rise of AI
16. Johns book is on the table
17. The package should arrive on Monday or Tuesday
18. I can't believe she said that
19. After the party we went to a restaurant
20. Did you finish your homework
21. He is a well known author
22. They are planning a trip to New York Boston and Washington DC
23. Please bring the following items a towel sunscreen and water
24. He asked What time is it
25. Its been a long day
26. The weather is great isn't it
27. She has lived in Paris France London England and Rome Italy
28. He said he would be there soon but he never showed up
29. The cake which was chocolate was delicious
30. Lets go out for dinner tonight

ARTICLES

Articles are words that define a noun as specific or unspecific. In English, there are two types of articles: definite and indefinite.

1. Definite Article: "The"

- **Usage:**

  - To refer to specific or known items: "The book on the table is mine."
  - When there is only one of something: "The sun is shining."
  - With superlatives: "She is the best student."
  - To refer to something previously mentioned: "I saw a dog. The dog was barking."

2. Indefinite Articles: "A" and "An"

- **Usage:**

  - To refer to a non-specific item: "I need a pen."
  - With singular, countable nouns: "She is reading a book."
  - "A" is used before words that begin with a consonant sound: "A cat."
  - "An" is used before words that begin with a vowel sound: "An apple."

3. Zero Article

- **Usage:**

  - With plural and uncountable nouns when speaking in general: "Books are important."
  - With most proper nouns: "He visited Paris."
  - With certain places and institutions (e.g., "at school," "in prison").

Practice Examples

Fill in the blanks with "a," "an," or "the" as appropriate.

1. She wants to buy ____ new car.
2. I saw ____ elephant at the zoo.
3. ____ book you gave me was interesting.
4. He is ____ honest man.

5. They live in ___ big house.
6. ___ sun rises in the east.
7. Can you pass me ___ salt, please?
8. I met ___ friend in the park.
9. She found ___ old coin in her backyard.
10. We are going to ___ beach this weekend.
11. He has ___ unique perspective on the matter.
12. She is wearing ___ beautiful dress.
13. I need ___ answer to my question.
14. ___ water in the lake is very cold.
15. He is looking for ___ job in finance.
16. She baked ___ cake for the party.
17. They are staying at ___ hotel downtown.
18. He has ___ interesting idea.
19. She visited ___ Eiffel Tower last summer.
20. I want to see ___ movie tonight.
21. She adopted ___ cat from the shelter.
22. He gave me ___ advice on my project.
23. There is ___ new student in our class.
24. She opened ___ window to let in some air.
25. He bought ___ apple and ___ orange.
26. ___ students were listening attentively.
27. She traveled to ___ Bahamas last year.
28. He drank ___ cup of coffee.
29. They are planning ___ trip to Europe.
30. She read ___ article about climate change.

PREPOSITIONS

Prepositions are words that show the relationship between a noun (or pronoun) and other words in a sentence. They usually indicate relationships of place, time, direction, or method.

1. Prepositions of Place

- **In**: Used for enclosed spaces or areas: "She is in the room."
- **On**: Used for surfaces or when something is on a line: "The book is on the table."
- **At**: Used for specific points or locations: "He is at the door."

2. Prepositions of Time

- **In**: Used for long periods (months, years, seasons): "She was born in 1990."
- **On**: Used for days and dates: "The meeting is on Monday."
- **At**: Used for specific times: "The party starts at 7 PM."

3. Prepositions of Direction

- **To**: Indicates movement toward a place: "He is going to the market."
- **Into**: Indicates movement into an enclosed space: "She walked into the room."
- **From**: Indicates the starting point of movement: "He came from the office."

4. Prepositions of Manner

- **By**: Indicates the method or means: "She traveled by train."
- **With**: Indicates using something or in the company of someone: "He wrote with a pen."
- **Like**: Indicates similarity: "He sings like a professional."

5. Prepositions of Possession

- **Of**: Indicates possession or connection: "The cover of the book is red."
- **With**: Indicates possession or feature: "The man with the blue shirt."

6. Prepositions of Cause, Reason, or Purpose

- **For**: Indicates purpose: "This is for you."
- **Because of**: Indicates reason: "She was late because of the traffic."

7. Prepositions of Agency

- **By**: Indicates the doer of an action in passive sentences: "The book was written by Orwell."

Practice Examples

Fill in the blanks with the correct preposition.

1. She sat ___ the chair.
2. He arrived ___ the airport.
3. The cat is ___ the table.
4. The concert starts ___ 8 PM.
5. She was born ___ April.
6. They walked ___ the park.
7. He put the keys ___ his pocket.
8. She came ___ the house.
9. The ball is ___ the box.
10. He is standing ___ the door.
11. She will meet us ___ Tuesday.
12. The car is parked ___ front of the building.
13. They are going ___ the movies tonight.
14. He wrote the letter ___ a pen.
15. She traveled ___ plane to London.
16. The picture hangs ___ the wall.
17. They moved ___ the city last year.
18. The event is scheduled ___ the afternoon.
19. The book is ___ the shelf.
20. She is talking ___ the phone.
21. The gift is ___ you.
22. The movie was directed ___ Spielberg.
23. He fell asleep ___ the meeting.
24. She lives ___ the second floor.
25. The plane flew ___ the clouds.
26. The kids are playing ___ the garden.
27. He is responsible ___ the project.
28. She walked ___ the bridge.
29. The phone is ___ the table.
30. They have been friends ___ childhood.

SUBJECT-VERB AGREEMENT

Subject-verb agreement is the grammatical rule that the verb must agree in number with its subject. This means that singular subjects take singular verbs, and plural subjects take plural verbs. Here are the main rules:

1. Singular and Plural Subjects

- Singular subjects take singular verbs: "The cat **is** sleeping."
- Plural subjects take plural verbs: "The cats **are** sleeping."

2. Subjects Joined by "And"

- When two or more subjects are joined by "and," they usually take a plural verb: "John and Mary **are** going to the store."
- Exception: If the compound subject refers to a single entity or idea, it takes a singular verb: "Peanut butter and jelly **is** my favorite snack."

3. Subjects Joined by "Or" or "Nor"

- When subjects are joined by "or" or "nor," the verb should agree with the subject closest to it: "Neither the teacher nor the students **are** ready."

4. Collective Nouns

- Collective nouns (e.g., team, group, family) can take either singular or plural verbs, depending on whether the group is seen as a single entity or as individuals:

  - "The team **is** winning." (as a single entity)
  - "The team **are** arguing among themselves." (as individuals)

5. Indefinite Pronouns

- Some indefinite pronouns (e.g., everyone, someone, each) are singular and take singular verbs: "Everyone **is** invited."
- Others (e.g., many, few, several) are plural and take plural verbs: "Many **are** coming to the party."

6. Subjects Separated from the Verb

- The subject is not always right next to the verb. Be careful to match the verb with the subject, not with a noun that comes in between: "The bouquet of roses **smells** lovely."

7. Titles, Names, and Other Singular Nouns

- Titles, company names, and other singular nouns take singular verbs: "Star Wars **is** a popular movie."

8. "There" and "Here" as Introductory Words

- When a sentence begins with "there" or "here," the verb agrees with the true subject that follows it: "There **are** two options."

9. Amount and Measurement

- Amount of money, time, distance, and measurements usually take singular verbs: "Five hundred rupees **is** enough."

10. Fractions and Percentages

- When a fraction or percentage is used, the verb agrees with the noun that follows it:

  - "One-third of the cake **is** gone."
  - "Forty percent of the students **are** absent."

Practice Examples
Choose the correct verb to complete each sentence.

1. The dog (barks/bark) at strangers.
2. Either my mother or my sisters (is/are) coming to the party.
3. The committee (has/have) made its decision.
4. Neither the teacher nor the students (is/are) ready.
5. The family (is/are) planning a vacation.
6. Mathematics (is/are) my favorite subject.
7. The jury (is/are) divided in their opinions.
8. Everyone (is/are) invited to the meeting.
9. A bouquet of flowers (makes/make) a lovely gift.
10. The news (is/are) on at 6 PM.
11. Here (is/are) the books you requested.
12. Five dollars (is/are) enough to buy the book.
13. The number of participants (has/have) increased.
14. The majority of the team (is/are) in agreement.

15. The police (is/are) investigating the case.
16. None of the students (has/have) completed the assignment.
17. One of the cars (is/are) parked illegally.
18. Bread and butter (is/are) all he wants for breakfast.
19. Two-thirds of the cake (was/were) eaten.
20. Either the manager or the employees (is/are) responsible for this.
21. Ten miles (is/are) a long distance to run.
22. Some of the cookies (has/have) been eaten.
23. Every one of the children (was/were) excited about the trip.
24. The team (is/are) celebrating their victory.
25. Half of the class (is/are) absent today.
26. John or his friends (is/are) going to the concert.
27. The audience (claps/clap) after every performance.
28. The pair of shoes (was/were) expensive.
29. The company (has/have) launched a new product.
30. Fifty percent of the votes (has/have) been counted.

www.ingramcontent.com/pod-product-compliance
Lightning Source LLC
Chambersburg PA
CBHW031758150726
47989CB00006B/2782